Resist and Masking Techniques

RESIST AND MASKING TECHNIQUES

Peter Beard

A & C Black · London

University of Pennsylvania Press · Philadelphia

First published in Great Britain 1996
A & C Black (Publishers) Limited
35 Bedford Row
London WC1R 4JH

ISBN 0–7136–3747–1

Published simultaneously in the US by:
University of Pennsylvania Press
423 Guardian Drive, Philadelphia, PA 19104

ISBN 0–8122–1611–3

Copyright © Peter Beard, 1996

Cover illustrations
front Vase by Peter Beard.

back Detail of a platter by Greg Daly (Australia).

Frontispiece Thrown vessel by Peter Beard (UK),
29 cm high. Multi-glaze layers on high and low
temperature glazes using a 'dot maker' of foam and
pantyhose.

Title page
The author's potter's mark. All potters, even
aspiring ones, should make their own seal mark
and then use it with discrimination.

Filmset in 10/12 Photina by August Filmsetting,
Haydock, St Helens
Printed in Hong Kong by
Wing King Tong Co. Ltd

Contents

Acknowledgements

Thank you to the following for their support and technical help:

Hilary Dawber, Phil Rogers, Ian Gower (photography), *Ceramic Monthly* Magazine (USA), T.C.A.S. Spray Equipment, Stoke on Trent City Museum and Library and all the artists and suppliers too numerous to mention who shared their knowledge and products.

Introduction

There are many simple and complicated processes used by ceramic artists and potters around the world. Each individual's work can be identified by his or her own style, which has evolved not only from his or her interest in particular forms, cultural influences and aesthetics but the study and development of particular techniques. These techniques from humble beginnings have been honed by practice and experimentation to become an integral and essential part of his or her expression. What are simple and sometimes obvious approaches become wondrous vehicles for the production of high quality work in the hands of the experienced. We have all, at some time in our lives, watched someone with high skills produce in what seems an effortless manner, an object before our eyes – only to find how difficult it is when we try it ourselves.

The work illustrated in this book conveys the results of these well-explored techniques. It was one of the first things that struck me while writing this book that stunning qualities are achieved over and over again but in many different ways using the same basic knowledge, and that these techniques are often very simple.

I intend to lead the reader whether he be complete novice, student, or professional looking for new avenues to explore, through the simplest of techniques on to the more complicated, showing what, with very little equipment or initial skills, interesting ceramic work can be achieved and, as confidence and understanding develop, how these areas can be widened and adapted to one's own individual statements. The processes in almost all cases are simple, but by exploring the use of slips, glazes and colours in conjunction with one or several resist or masking techniques I hope you will extend your knowledge and enjoyment of that medium we call ceramics.

L to R   Plate, black ground with gold lustre, Staffordshire bone china, 1828–30. Ground laid black background resisted with sugar water.

Teapot, blue and white, cobalt dusted colour through paper or vellum mask to form panels for decoration. Bow porcelain 1775.

Dish, tin-glazed earthenware, Bristol or Wincanton 1750–60. Manganese dioxide dusted through vellum mask to form panels for decoration. *Courtesy of the Stoke on Trent City Museum.*

Chapter One
History and Overview of Resists and Masking

Early decoration

When centuries ago an Aborigine placed his hand on a rock and sprayed ochre earth from his mouth over its surface to reveal the hand shape below, a simple mask had been used. Although not a ceramic event, the idea of a mask was realised. Pottery developed as we all know from plain, simple pinch and coil pots with no use of pattern onto pots decorated with the addition of simple patterns made by carving techniques and impressing found objects.

Over the centuries, the sophistication of form and decoration developed along with firing techniques. However, the use of masks does not appear to have been an avenue explored at all widely by early potters. Even the development of slips and glazes and the discovery of colouring oxides did not help to open up this area. Decorating techniques still utilised the finger drawn through slip, slip trailing, carving and scratching and the use of the brush. For instance, the Greeks in 400–300 BC were making very sophisticated 'Black Figure Ware' with intricately executed brush painting using colloidal slips that responded to the action of smoke in a carefully controlled reduction firing to give the well-known black and red figure ware.

During an oxidising firing the atmosphere in the kiln is kept clear and the flame gives off CO_2 and heats up the pots without any special effect on the oxygen content of the clay. In a reduction firing the flame does not receive enough oxygen for complete combustion and gives off CO. In an attempt to get more oxygen, the flame draws it from the clay, where the oxygen is in the form of metal oxides. As oxygen is drawn out, the metal is released causing the clay to change colour. The colloidal slip favoured by the Greeks was rich in iron and so turned black in the reduction firing. The dense nature of colloidal slips means that they sinter at a lower temperature than the main clay body of the vessel, 850°C in this case. The kiln was then oxidised and the body of the pot which had also turned black reoxidised and turned red, because the clay body of the pot was of a more open texture, and therefore had a higher maturing temperature. It had not sintered like the now 'sealed' slip which remained black. Hence black figures on a red ground. It could be said that the slip was masking out the clay below, but in reality the Greeks were just utilising the ability of the slip to go black more easily than the body. I mention this here as it will be seen in the text later how artists today do use this property of colloidal slip as a type of mask.

Masks and resists

It was not until the introduction of mass-produced ware for a worldwide market in the late 17th and early 18th century with the development of tin-glazed earthenware and porcelains that the use of masks and resists began to appear. The triggering factor appears to have been the development of a wide range of colours for underglaze and onglaze decoration in both earthenware and porcelain. This occurred primarily in ceramic centres such as Stoke-on-Trent in England.

The use of colouring oxides such as copper, iron, and manganese had been well-exploited but there was also a need for a wider range of colours to satisfy the rapidly growing sophistication of the potteries' customers. This demand was fuelled by the import of brightly coloured ware from China. By the early 18th century, the science of colour production was well under way but each factory had its own colour shop for its own internal consumption. In the late 1700s colour makers began to leave the factories and set up their own businesses to supply the industry.

The types of colouring used were split into four main groups: *Underglaze colours*, which as the name suggests, were painted on the bisque ware, glazed and then fired. *Coloured glazes* which were painted on the bisque ware and on already glazed but not fired surfaces. *Maiolica, delftware or tin-glazed earthenware* where the colours were applied onto a layer of unfired white tin glaze. Finally, *enamel colours* that were painted onto a previously fired glaze surface. The enamel colours could be lower fired than the base glaze (as long as they would fuse onto the surface), thereby giving a wide range of colours as some more delicate colours would fade at high temperatures.

The development of a wide palette of colours with such evocative names as Purple of Cassius (gold dissolved in aqua regia, giving pinks to purples) meant that much more elaborate decoration was possible and in turn, required by the public. The earlier work was decorated mainly by brush for both wide areas of colour and more detailed pictorial scenes and flowers. Although the application of wide blocks of colour particularly in cobalt blue by brush gave good results, the flatness of the colour was only possible with great skill. The addition of various oils – to make the colour flow better – helped, but the result was not always as desired.

As the demand for more and more work of a consistent quality increased, it became desirable to develop quicker ways of production with higher standards of quality. It was at this stage that masking and resist techniques began to appear. Because in the pottery industry skills were passed on from master to apprentice, there was very little need to write down any methods of executing work and for this reason there is very little early documentation available. Luckily, some techniques in the industry for very high quality hand-decorated work are still utilised today. In my research, the earliest definite use of masking as a regular method that I could find was in 1750 (see photograph on page 8). At that time, it was fashionable to cover large areas of the piece in a flat colour leaving white panels that could then be painted by brush with scenes and pictures of flora. This piece illustrated is a tin-glazed earthenware dish made in Bristol or Wincanton, England on which vellum cut-out shapes were laid and the whole dish dusted with manganese powder. Because the manganese colour would spread only slightly in the glaze during firing, the masking did not need to be too accurate. So, the stiff mask did not need to be fixed too tightly to the surface to prevent the powder creeping under it and if executed vertically above the piece little creep would occur anyway.

Some pieces that needed large areas of more than one colour before brush decoration exploited the water-resisting qualities of animal fats. The term for preventing the contamination of one area of colour with another was called 'stopping'. Oils of various kinds had been tried but they tended to absorb into the bisque unevenly and so did not give consistent results. Melted mutton suet was used to give perfect sharpness.

The area to have the first colour would be drawn out with carbon while the remaining areas were liberally coated with fat. It was important to be to careful to get a crisp edge and not to put any grease on the areas to be coloured. Dipping was the usual method of applying the colour, but brushing would work too, as long as the fat set fairly stiff and could not be smudged with the brush stroke. After the first application, the ware would be heated to a point where the fat would volatilise and the piece no longer resisted. This had the added advantage of setting the first colour so that it would be less likely to smudge when handled. The previously applied colour and any areas to be left clear for detailed painting could then be stopped for the second colour application. Not a profession for vegetarians!

There were still factories who applied colour all over a piece and then laboriously scraped away the areas to be left white. This was time-consuming and any small amount of colour not removed would show after firing. This method was most prevalent in German factories.

At this time flat colour areas for both bisque and onglaze were being applied by brush, dusting, dipping, splattering (flicking the colour and medium from a stiff brush) and a process known as ground laying. Ground laying allowed large areas of completely flat colour to be applied to the ware. It had already been discovered that the addition of oils, both natural and manmade, when added to the pigment would allow the brush to flow more easily giving more fluid and intricate brush work. Many of these oils, from nut oils to oil of turpentine, could be boiled to make them more viscous. Also, after decoration, they could be heated to stiffen them so that the decoration would remain 'fast' while being handled.

Ground laying gave a much more professional, machine-like finish to the work and was a highly skilled operation. The area to be coloured was painted with oil of turpentine and dabbed with a pad of lint-free soft cloth until the oil formed an even, sticky layer. Another ball of cloth was used to pick up dry, powdered colour which was then dabbed repeatedly all over the oil thereby depositing a layer of colour. The colour continued to be applied until the oil could absorb no more. This would result, when fired, in a perfectly flat, even coat. The oil had to be just right for it to be dabbed into an even coat and for it not to lift off onto the colour applicator. The problem was that when the dabbing procedure was executed, the oil and colour would spread beyond the designated area. To avoid this, a mixture of sugar and water mixed with rose pink, an identifying dye, was painted on the area to be left clean. This was allowed to dry and the whole piece was covered in the oil and ground laid. The piece was then immersed in clean water and agitated which dissolved the sugar water or 'stencil' as it is known and the unwanted ground laying could be removed with fine, loose cotton wool. Care had to be taken to keep the whole piece immersed until the operation was complete so that the unwanted colour would not restick back onto the wrong areas. This method of masking is still used today in the industry for high quality, hand-decorated ware. The sugar normally used is golden syrup. Ground laying was the most commonly used masking technique before the invention of ceramic colour printing and transfers. Sugar water was also used as a medium for underglaze painting on bisque ware.

Lustreware, popular in the early 19th century, used resists made from a mixture of jewellers rouge and clay although the proportions are not recorded. It was important that a mixture was used that was soluble in water to facilitate its removal after the low firing and to help the masking from the oil-based lustre. Other mixtures using gums, honey, sugar, and glycerine with vermilion watercolour paint are recorded. Vermilion was a yellow vegetable dye that would not leave a permanent stain on the ware but helped to guide the decorators. Chinese white watercolour paint tinted with crimson lake and even today household white emulsion paint have been used. The liquid lustre was applied to the ware, with resisting medium already in the required areas, either by painting or dipping. The ware was fired and the resist medium was then washed from the pot with cotton wool and water. There is more detail about the lustre masking used today later in the book.

Other techniques employed to mask out colour that had been splattered and flicked to form a coloured ground, relied on the fact that gum arabic shrinks slightly when heated. Two main methods were common. The first employed a mixture of gum and chalk applied as a paste to the areas to be left blank. The colour mixed with oil was then splattered all over the piece which was in turn warmed to fix the colour and also to cause the gum/chalk mixture to shrink which would loosen the mask. This would then easily flake away leaving the ground clean. In the second method the colour was applied first then the chalk and paste mix smeared onto the areas to be blank. The ware was then heated as before and, as the paste shrank, it would fall away taking the colour with it. Any slight residues left could be scraped away. The latter method was apparently quicker and therefore preferred in the industry.

Stencils made of thin sheets of metal, either zinc or copper, or of oiled paper were used to help repeat designs on a run of ware. The colour could be dusted through these stencils onto oils which had been previously applied to the ware or the oil could be applied with the stencil and then the colour dusted on. Sponges loaded with colour to give a textured appearance were also employed and several stencils could be used for one design. If several colours and stencils were to be used, the colour would contain either gums or oils that could be heated to harden the preceding application.

Stencils were often employed to lay down the outline of a repeat design for the decorator to follow. These had the outlines marked in them as either a series of holes or slits through which powdered charcoal was dusted. The image left by the powdery charcoal could then be outlined in rose water to be more permanent. This type of stencil was called a pounce.

As the industry developed and ware

had to be produced at a faster and faster rate to satisfy demand, quicker methods of decoration were sought. Copperplate printing began in England in 1750 with early experiments on a one colour image. The process involved either the hand engraving of copperplates with the design or later acid etching the plate. Ceramic colour in an oil medium was coated on the plate making sure it went fully into the grooves of the design. The excess on the surface was removed, a sheet of paper laid on the surface and the plate was passed through a press to pick

Acid etched plate with burnished gold. 1) Pattern printed in rubber solution. 2) Large areas to be resisted masked out in rubber solution. 3) Glazed surface etched with acid, mask removed. 4) Gold lustre painted on patterned surface. 5) Fired gold. 6) Raised surface of pattern burnished to reveal pattern as matt and bright areas. *Courtesy of the Stoke on Trent City Museum.*

up the design on the paper. This paper with its sticky print could then be laid on the ware face down and by gentle rubbing the design could be persuaded to stick to the surface. The paper was then soaked in water to remove it, the ceramic colour in oil not being affected.

This method could only produce one print at time in one colour and it was not until the invention of paper as a continuous roll in 1831 that printing machines were developed to create mass-produced designs on a large scale. Further inventions came very quickly as demand increased for multi-coloured images to be developed.

One technique employed by a French company to apply a design from an engraved copperplate onto the ware is worthy of a mention. It is not in itself a masking or resisting technique but it may spark someone's desire to experiment in conjunction with other methods described later in the book. I hasten to add using modern alternative materials! A solution of 'Flanders glue' or gelatine was prepared by boiling the clippings of glove leather and parchment into a consistency of thick syrup. This was poured while still warm onto a flat metal sheet and allowed to cool, giving a sheet of gel 3 mm ($\frac{1}{8}$ inch) thick with the consistency of rubber. The copperplate was 'inked' with a boiled, drying, nut oil mixed with a little essence of turpentine. The plate was wiped off in the usual way leaving the oil in the grooves of the design. The gelatine sheet was carefully laid on the plate and pressed down evenly to pick up the oil. The sheet was then removed and placed on the bisque flat ware. There the oil image stuck very sharply and could be dusted with very finely ground dry colour using the finest carded cotton wool, and the image appeared.

It was discovered that gelatine swells uniformly in cold water (before dissolving) and shrinks evenly if immersed in alcohol. In water it swells to a third larger. This knowledge was utilised to make enlargements and reductions to the engraving's size so the same image could be used for a range of ware. I can imagine someone today developing an interesting range of work using transferred oil prints as a resisting tool.

With the invention of lithography, developed mainly in France, and photography, sophisticated multi-coloured transfers became the norm, as it is in the ceramic industry we know today.

As the mechanisation of colour production developed so the need for masking and resist techniques diminished. Today they are used in the ceramic industry on only very high quality hand-painted tableware and then only in a limited fashion.

Acid etching of glazed ware was used extensively in the past as a means of dissolving away areas of glaze contaminated with an incorrect colour to allow reglazing to turn a 'second' back into a 'first'. It was also and still is used to create a three-dimensional pattern in the glaze prior to gilding in precious metal. A pattern is either hand painted or printed directly onto the ware in rubber solution that will not be affected by the acid. Any other areas not to be touched by the acid are blanked out. When dry, the piece is immersed in hydrofluoric acid to bite into the glaze where needed. Hydrofluoric acid is the only acid that will attack glass (glaze) and is extremely dangerous – much more so than many other acids. On removal and washing, the rubber mask can be removed revealing the pattern. The gold can be painted over the etched area, fired, then polished only on the high glaze points leaving the pattern revealed in matt and polished gold. Acid has also been used with the rubber masks to matt glazed surfaces in patterns and lettering.

Sandblasting or grit blasting has been used to 'blow away' areas of glaze down to the bisque to create panels for redecoration. A stream of fine abrasive material is sprayed through stencils at high speed onto the ware and the particles wear away the glaze layer. Thin metal sheets or thick paper are used as their relative softness absorbs the abrasive quality of the grit and they don't disintegrate too quickly. Sandblasting will be covered more fully later in the book.

Glaze sprayed through simple stencils to produce, for example, different coloured lettering was also used although nowadays transfers would be simplest solution.

Chapter Two
Water-based Waxes

Water-based wax comes in a standard liquid form and is usually ready to use. In some cases dilution of the wax with water may be desirable if a less defined patterning is required. Although most waxes are of a similar composition, they do vary in strength from country to country so it is best to satisfy yourself that your wax is appropriate for your intended application.

Water-based wax is usually made up of oil-water emulsions based on a mixture of wax, water and Vaseline (petroleum jelly). All have a shelf life and must be protected from freezing. Wax emulsion is non-toxic but it does cause a slight skin irritation with prolonged contact. Water-based waxes are usually best suited for use on dry clay, bisque, unfired and fired glaze surfaces. In fact, in any circumstances where adhesive masks won't stick, i.e. damp or dusty surfaces, and where more freehand marks are required. Damp clay surfaces can be a problem as the water in the wax has difficulty evaporating.

In most cases the wax appears as a white or pale beige liquid that, once painted on, becomes translucent, making it difficult to see, especially when the patterning is fine and intricate. This problem can be overcome by the addition of food colouring, readily available from any food store. The addition of food colouring does not in any way affect the resisting properties of the wax. Different colours can be used when building up layer over layer to differentiate between patterns. The translucency of dry wax allows guidelines to be drawn in either pencil or food colouring depending on the surface. It also allows the ceramicist to see below the surface to see if further texturing, i.e. scratching through the wax surface is needed.

For the wax to work effectively, it is important that it is allowed to dry completely before applying the layer that

Flat vessel by Peter Beard (UK), 29 cm high. Using water-based wax with different coloured glazes to create patterns.

is to be resisted. Failure to do this will result in a blurred image or no image at all. Drying in normal conditions is only a few minutes as the fired or dry clay readily absorbs and dissipates the moisture. If you are trying to create patterns on wet or leatherhard clay, the water in the wax may not work so effectively. In such a situation it is better to use latex wax or hot wax.

Shaped home-made brushes for quick application. Top left flattened brush with bristle removed, bottom left tufts of bristle glued into convex piece of wood for the inside of bowls. Right concave piece of wood with tufts of bristles glued in for the outside of cylinder shapes.

Methods of application

Brushes

The most common method of application of water-based wax is by brush. If the brush is in continual use you should be careful that it does not become clogged. If you are working intermittently on a piece or pieces of work, then it is advisable to stand the brush in water when it is not in use. This will prevent it drying out. However, do remember to remove any excess water before commencing work again, otherwise the first strokes will contain too diluted a wax to be effective. Note: brushes made of manmade fibres clog much more easily than natural hairs. This is

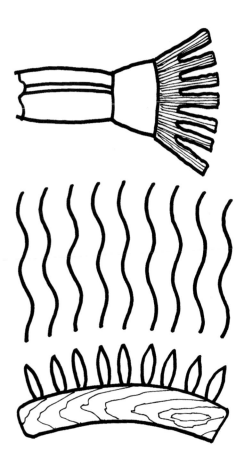

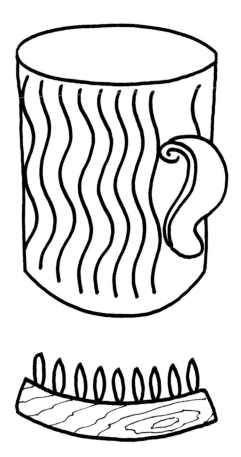

particularly true when applying wax to an unfired glaze surface as the stiffer bristles tend to scratch off small quantities of powdered glaze which sticks and builds up in the brush. Brushes that become clogged should be allowed to dry and then stood in white spirit for an hour, then washed in detergent and hot water. This is the same procedure for any tools where wax has become dried on.

With a brush you are normally only able to make single lines. However, if quick application of a series of similar lines is required, say, on domestic ware where quick production is important, it is quite easy to make up brushes with multiple heads. The first method is to take a fat brush, say 12 mm ($\frac{1}{2}$ inch) diameter, and to hammer the metal collar that holds the bristles flat. This will cause the bristles to splay out in a fan shape. Using scissors or a sharp craft knife, areas of bristle can be removed at regular intervals forming what is essentially a multi-headed brush. If the

top end of the bristle head is cut either in a slight concave or convex manner, it can be used in the first case for the exterior of, for example, mugs and in the second case, the interior of bowls. If a large area is to be covered with one stroke, then tufts of brush hair can be glued into holes in a suitably formed piece of wood. Fan-shaped brushes are available from pottery suppliers. They are called 'fan blenders' and they can be cut to shape.

Sponge and foam applications

Intricate patterns can be repeatedly applied using upholstery foam stamps which have the design cut into them. The piece of foam should be big enough to be carefully held without squashing the pattern when in use. Because it is very difficult to cut patterns in the surface of foam due to its flexibility, the following methods are recommended:

The easiest way to create sponge

Left
Various sponges cut with hot wires and tubes, the bottom is the foam packing used to sell coloured chalks. The wax used is water-based coloured with food dye.

Patterned sponge painting rollers made with hot wire and tube. Stained wax rolled on tiles.

Below
Black enamel painted on the wax.

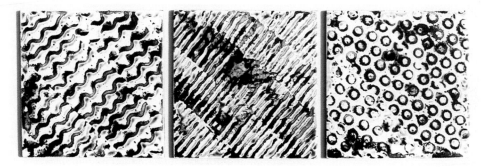

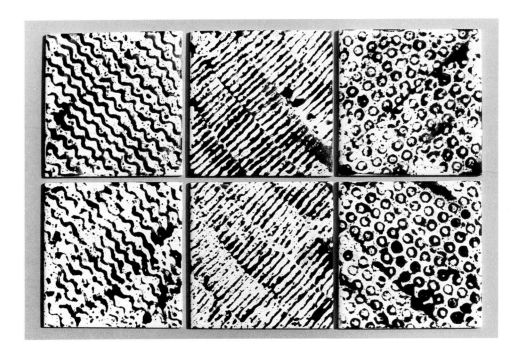

Fired result.

patterns is to draw the intended design on the sponge surface. Then, using a hot soldering iron tip or a metal rod that has been heated to red heat, burn away the foam that is not needed. Dot patterns can be formed using heated metal tubes of differing sizes touched on to the surface of the foam. The foam burns very easily so care must be taken to use a light, quick touch. Note: the fumes given off from burning foam are VERY toxic and the process should only be undertaken with suitable extraction facilities. The gases contain large quantities of cyanide as well as other extremely dangerous chemicals.

If suitable extraction facilities are not available, then draw out the design on the foam with a waterproof pen. Soak the sponge in water, wring out the excess so that the sponge is still damp and put it in the deep freeze until frozen. Then, with a sharp craft knife, carefully cut the excess foam away from the now stiff foam. If the sponge begins to defrost before the cutting is complete, then simply return it to the deep freeze until it is refrozen.

Techniques of sponge application

Patterned sponges used for water-based wax are best dampened before dipping in wax. This helps to get a good, even coating on the sponge before pressing it on to the object to be decorated. It is best to allow excess wax to run off before application and then not to press too hard or the wax absorbed up into the foam will run or flow into areas that are supposed to stay bare.

When using sponges on convex surfaces, a rolling action is needed. When applying on concave surfaces, the sponge should be squeezed at the rear so that the patterned surface forms a slight concave surface. This will then make even contact. Otherwise, a poorly defined patterning will result. It is difficult to go over an area if the wax is not applied properly the first time.

As pressure is applied to the sponge against the surface being decorated, the patterned surface will compress and be slightly distorted. The more pressure, the more distortion. For this reason it is best not to cut the pattern in the sponge too deeply, especially if it is a fine one, as the movement of the sponge can cause the printing area to become so distorted that it destroys the pattern in wax, resulting in a large wax smudge. A depth of no more than 10 mm ($\frac{3}{8}$ inch) is best. However, too shallow a pattern will result in wax filling everything, again destroying the wax print.

A small piece of foam wrapped tightly in pantyhose to form a ball attached to a stick or wire makes an excellent tool for making dots and the harder it is pressed, the larger dot it makes.

Sponges should be cleaned in water immediately after use and washed between uses if being employed intermittently on one piece. The foam is difficult to clean if wax has dried on it. Its pores become blocked so it will not soak up wax and it will have to be remade. Foam, if stored in a squashed condition for long periods, will remain in its distorted shape for a long time (sometimes days), once the sponge is released from its pressure. It is therefore important to store it carefully and loosely, not stuffed in a drawer. Modern foams are designed to break down in the environment and are affected by daylight so store your cut foam and stock foam in darkness. What happens is that the outer surface goes hard and friable and

powdery, so hard edges become rounded. This process does take months, sometimes years, but having stored my own sponges on a windowsill only to find them useless when I needed them, I have since been more careful.

Points to watch for

Although water-based wax does dry, it still retains a slight stickiness so you can use a pencil eraser or your finger to remove mistakes on dry clay and unfired glaze. You do this by pressing your finger or pencil eraser lightly on the wax in a dabbing motion and the wax layer should stick to your finger and lift off. In using this method, it is important that the wax has been allowed to dry or the water content will be too high and the

Sponging waxed surface to erode surrounding clay leaving a relief pattern.
Photograph by Ruth E. Allan.

wax too soft to stick and lift off. This method is not suitable with hot wax. If the wax has been painted onto green ware, it is possible to carefully scratch away any mistakes as long as they are small. Mistakes on bisque ware are much more difficult to remove and usually the only solution is to refire the piece in your next bisque firing or to fire the piece to 600°C to burn off the wax and then start again.

A common mistake with wax is running. This is caused by an overloaded brush or by pressing the brush too hard. With a water-based wax, a light touch is all that is needed.

When using water-based wax, if the unfired glaze layer to be decorated has been allowed to dry too long, say for a full day before waxing, it is likely that it will lift, causing crawling during firing. This is caused by the water in the wax as it passes through the dry glazed layer to the bisque below. It is better to decorate directly after glazing as long as the glaze has appeared to dry but still retains some moisture. A little dampness is always best.

Other water-based wax techniques

Waxes, paper and tapes

Water-based waxes and hot waxes can be used with paper and tape masks to form crisp, geometric results in situations where paper and tapes alone, more usually employed for very accurate work, do not work so well i.e. damp or powdery surfaces. Waxes are less suited to create very hard edged work as they have a tendency to flow. If waxes are required or are preferred, then paper or tapes cut to shape can be applied to a surface, the whole area covered in wax,

the paper then removed revealing the surface below, very crisp, which can then be coated in pigment which takes only where the paper was.

Wax and shellac

Wax can be used on unfired clay to act as a mask whilst the surrounding clay is eroded with water to form a relief (see Ruth E. Allen in the Smoke section). However, it is more common to use shellac which is a type of natural varnish. This technique has been used to great effect by Jeroen Bechtold.

Jeroen Bechtold (Holland)

Jeroen Bechtold works in porcelain and by using masks and water refines the thickness of his forms to allow light to reveal, when fired, the translucency and details of the pattern created.

The forms are slipcast quite thick and allowed to dry out completely. The patterns are areas blocked out with shellac, which is a resinous substance secreted by the lac insect and dissolved in alcohol. Any natural or manmade varnish will work but Jeroen, after experimentation, prefers shellac.

Once the shellac has dried, the vessel is sponged with a wet natural sponge to wash and erode the areas which are not coated. The patterns are blocked out on both the inside and outside of the form. The erosion of the unmasked clay begins to leave different thicknesses which eventually, when fired, will allow the passage of light.

After a time the cast has absorbed so much water that it begins to soften. This is the time to stop. Leave the cast to dry thoroughly. Later further sponging can take place on the same areas. Once the desired thicknesses have been achieved,

'He who catches clouds' by Jeroen Bechtold (Holland). Porcelain with shellac painted patterns, water etched. *Photograph by Rene Gerritsen.*

Right
Block Vessel by Peter Beard, 46 cm high. Water-based wax decoration, high and low temperature glazes, stoneware.

the shellac mask can be removed by light sponging with alcohol or new areas can be blocked out and the process continued.

The advantage of shellac over other varnishes is that it can be dissolved once dry. Other materials have to be scraped or peeled away which could damage the crispness of the design. Others could possibly be fired away without any problem.

Because the cast in its unfired state is

23

not as translucent as it will be when fired, the skill is in knowing when to stop so that the wall does not become so thin that it fails but at the same time is thin enough that the passage of light is sufficient to give a pleasing result. As the walls become thinner, the water passes more quickly through the thinner areas and this shows as a darkening of the dry clay. In time one can judge the thickness by the darkness of the clay.

Sponging leaves the masked area as a hard-edged island and in Jeroen's work the difficulty and skill is in lining up the outside thicker areas with the inside ones so that when light passes through the vessel they contrast against each other in the desired alignment. The failure rate for his work is very high as the thickness of wall needed to show through the maximum light is very thin. He has tried using steel wool to wear away the clay but it is not as controllable as with water and there is the dust problem. If too much work is done on an area, the shellac sometimes softens and cracks and as with so many techniques practice gives the knowledge for the correct control of the process.

Peter Beard (UK)

My work is a mixture of handbuilt and thrown forms, some vessel based. I use a small range of base glazes to which are added oxides and ceramic pigments so that I have a wide palette of colour to use but with similar surface qualities. Some of these glazes are matt stoneware glazes and some high shine earthenware glazes but I fire all my work to 1280°C causing some glazes to overflux and react strongly with the other glazes either over, under or nearby.

The glazes are applied in layers by a mixture of pouring, spraying, dipping and brushing depending on the finished texture I wish to achieve. I use almost exclusively water-base wax slightly diluted and stained with food colouring so that it is easier to follow on the work. The wax is painted on to the base glaze coating, in the required pattern, allowed to dry to achieve its maximum resistance before applying, with a brush, other layers of glaze.

The final layers of glaze are built up to the required thickness in several coats, either of the same colour or of several colours. The pieces are then allowed to dry before firing. Care is taken to build up the layers slowly so that the wax will retain its resisting qualities and not be overrun with a too viscous glaze. Some droplets remain on the surface of the wax and I leave these to soften the appearance of the surface.

The final result of either a hard pattern or a more fluid surface is dependent on the glaze thickness. All the decoration and subsequent application of glazes must be done when the work is damp otherwise it will flake away in sheets during the final firing – the water introduced causing the first glaze to lose its grip on the surface.

Rimas VisGirda (USA)

Rimas VisGirda's work, with its strong graphic images, is built from either stoneware or earthenware clay and sometimes a mixture of the two. They are decorated when either bone dry or after bisque firing.

Each piece has a layer of engobe painted over the surface and because this layer shrinks as it dries, the result is a texture of tiny cracks, similar to that seen at the bottom of dry river beds. The thicker the engobe, the more, larger and severe the cracks.

'Burro Brand' by Jeff Irwin (USA), 9 inches high. Decorated using black and white engobe and water-based wax.

It is worth noting that the fit of the engobe to the clay below has to be such that any other shrinkage that takes place in subsequent firings does not result in the engobe flaking off. As a rule, the thicker the engobe layer, the more likely this is to happen but the more dramatic the cracking. All slips and engobes can be made to do this with practice, and with the addition of a small amount of flux to a slip if it is not already in the recipe, flaking can be avoided.

After the engobe has dried, the design is carefully drawn on the surface with a soft pencil. The entire piece is then coated in wax emulsion. It is important that the wax layer is thick enough that it will resist well but still allow the drawn design to show through. Some waxes that are more opaque than others will have to be diluted. Rimas uses 'green wax', 'white wax', 'Ceramul' and other brand wax emulsions. (Latex wax is not suitable for drawing through because of its rubbery nature.)

The lines of the drawing are followed, scratching through the wax and the engobe layer to the clay body below, after which they are flooded with an oxide-heavy, black engobe resulting in his characteristic black outlined images.

It is important that the work is in the correct condition for the scratching to be crisp and even. If there is too much moisture in the object, the wax may not dry completely and so it will not resist properly. Then, when the lines are drawn, the tool may produce a mushy furrow. If the wax does not resist well even though the engobe is at the correct stage to be scratched, then Rimas draws the pattern and leaves the piece to dry to the point where the wax achieves the necessary properties. A wax emulsion that appears to be thick enough but does not resist well is usually caused by too much dampness in the object. A piece coated in wax will take quite a long time to dry because of the wax's waterproofing qualities.

If too dry, the lines appear shallow and scratchy and the engobe can lift at the edges. Also, the clay dust can stick to the wax reducing its resisting properties. A solution to both these problems is to gently sponge the surface with a damp, natural sponge to soften the engobe and make it stick back down and to wash away the dust.

The piece is then fired to the maturing temperature of the body cone 05. The surface is coated with a satin glaze, sponged off, so that it fills the cracks in the surface and is refired. Colour shading is added with underglaze pencils, liquid underglazes and lustres. A firing is needed for each colour application before the piece is finished.

Left
'The car we bought together just began to rust' by Rimas Visgirda (USA), 24 inches high. Decorated using engobes, underglaze pencils and china paints. Water-based wax used to resist colour areas.

Chapter Three
Oil-based Waxes

Hot wax is basically paraffin wax or candle wax that has been gently heated until it has melted. It is particularly useful on very damp surfaces where a water-based wax would not dry.

Hot wax on its own cools and solidifies too quickly to be of any practical use. Indeed, by the time the brush with the melted wax has reached the object, the wax has usually solidified. However, the addition of either paraffin oil/kerosine or machine oil will dilute the wax, making it more fluid so that it will continue to flow at a much lower temperature. Small amounts of cooking oil can also be used. The amount of paraffin to be added depends on the application but a 50:50 mix would be a good starting point. It must be remembered that as more oil or kerosine is added, the wax will become softer. If too much is added, the wax will become a greasy liquid that is of no practical use. Commercially available liquid wax floor polishes can also be tried but they don't need heating.

Application

Hot wax is usually applied by brushing. It is important to get the right consistency of hot wax for each individual application. Testing is the best way to determine the correct consistency. However, as a general rule, you should be aiming to achieve the hardest of coatings with the greatest fluidity for application. Harder drying mixtures are better for waxing bases and lids whilst the softer end of the scale is more useful for brushwork as a more fluid line can be achieved.

Preparation

To make a wax mixture, the candle wax is melted in a suitable container over a low flame or electric ring with a thermostat. The oil is slowly added and the two are stirred together. It must be remembered that these are inflammable materials; the heating should be gentle and safety measures should be at hand to extinguish this type of fat fire should an accident occur. I would recommend that an electric, thermostatically controlled heat source always be used as this will greatly reduce the risk of fire. An electric frying pan is ideal. Whilst the wax and other materials are being mixed, there should be no evidence of smoke or vapour. If this occurs, the mixture is too hot.

Wax of this type is usually made in the container that it will be stored in and used from. After use it can just be left to cool until the next time it is needed. The wax does not deteriorate if the container is left open unless it is not used for very long periods during which time some of the oil may evaporate. However, this can be easily replaced at the next melting.

Applying slips and glazes

When applying a slip or a glaze to a waxed area, a brush can be used. However, the brush may tend to smudge the soft wax, thereby damaging the original image. Dipping is the best method of applicaiton but spraying is a possible alternative. However, the spray can dry significantly in the air before it reaches the ceramic surface. It may then stick to the waxed area which will necessitate laborious and careful sponging to remove it. (See Spraying on Page 44.)

Wax crayons

Wax crayons for drawing on bisque or fired glazed ware can be made from candle wax. However, they are generally too hard to be used on green ware or unfired glaze unless the object is robust or the glaze has been made into a suitable crust with the addition of a gum or starch, e.g. gum arabic, cornstarch or CMC, or has had a hardening on firing. Applied glaze can be pre-fired to bisque temperatures to render it a sintered crust for crayon drawing, but you must establish if your glaze will be affected by

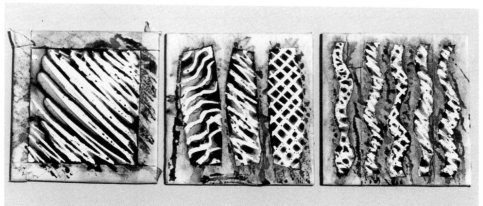

Top
Tiles masked with masking tape and patterned with black wax crayon to show up in photograph.

Above
Tiles patterned with candle wax then painted with black enamel.

this when refired to its maturing temperature as glaze crawling can occur. If crayons are required for these conditions, then paraffin must be added as described above to make them softer.

Ceramic pigments, i.e. oxides or enamels, can be added to the crayons so that it is possible to draw in coloured lines which will also resist. Four parts wax to one part dry pigment to one part oil should be melted together, stirring well. Then the molten mixture can be poured into a cardboard or paper tube stuck into clay, or poured into the fingers of a rubber glove. It will be found that because the pigment is heavier than the liquid, it will sometimes settle out, making one end of the crayon stronger in pigment than the other. If the tube mould is waterproof, standing it in cold water whilst pouring in the wax will encourage quick solidification and hence alleviate settlement problems. It may be

found that candle wax is too crumbly for some applications and the addition of excess paraffin can make the crayons too slimy. If this is the case, beeswax and linseed oil is a good alternative. The proportions needed depend upon your preference but a mixture of one part oil to two parts beeswax is a good starting point. Again, the wax and oil are gently heated together and pigment added as required; again, fast cooling prevents settlement. The pigments used should be sieved through a fine sieve or ground in a ball mill to make sure of an even colour. These crayons are very versatile and can be used, of course, without pigments. Those wax crayons containing enamels are particularly useful for drawing on glazed ware, either on their own or with washes of other enamel colours. They draw a fuzzy edged line and give a tonal quality when used loosely to fill in an area similar to art wax pastels on textured paper.

Wax litho crayons which are free of

Tape masks removed and fired results.

pigment can be bought from good
quality art suppliers and come in a range
of hardnesses. Very successful results can
be achieved with the commercially-made
wax crayons and pastels used for non-
ceramic drawing. They are generally soft
enough for use on work at most stages.
It will be found that the pigments used in
their manufacture do not always fire out.
This is particularly true with the earth
tones, flesh colours and white. These

Bottle Form by Brian Trueman (UK). Hot wax
used to create panels of different glazes. Hot
wax then used for fine detailing and further
application of colour.

leave varying degrees of colour from
dark iron browns through tans to cream.
At high temperatures they become
permanently adhered to the body. Oil
pastels have an immediate appeal in the
ease of application to the bisque body

and lend themselves to a loose, spontaneous approach. They can be used in conjunction with stencils and adhesive tape for a harder edged format with a textured infill.

As oil pastels are of a soft, greasy nature, you can work the medium after application. They can be easily smudged and merged to give tonal qualities in the final piece from your added or already present pigments. Areas crayoned can be scratched through for fine line drawing. They resist liquids very well and marks made will reproduce well in the finished piece.

The disadvantage of bought pastels is their limited fired colour range, but used in conjunction with homemade ones, a wide palette is possible. At low temperatures, the pigments will not always adhere to the surface. If using bought pastels, buy a box with a wide colour range from a company that also sells the colours separately in order that the colours most frequently used can easily be replaced.

Slip trailing with hot wax

Slip trailing with water-based waxes is not really possible as the material is too fluid, and even on horizontal surfaces tends to run. Careful preparation of a hot wax mixture is more feasible. As described already, the paraffin wax is melted and the kerosine is added and allowed to cool. The result should be a thick paste. This can be stored in jars for later use. To render the paste usable, remove a quantity into another jar and add more kerosine and shake well until the wax is almost liquid. Any lumps that are difficult to remove should be sieved out through a course mesh. The wax should be stiffish, trailable but not liquid. Draw the wax up into a slip trailer and

gently shake it down in the trailer to remove any air pockets. Then begin work. Note: the slip trailer can be cleaned with kerosine but in time this will ruin the tool as kerosine reacts with some rubber and plastics.

The mixture can be trailed very easily as it does not need heat to make it flow. It repels glaze extremely well, leaving a good, clear mark. There is very little retention of glaze on the wax surface. The disadvantages are that the mixture is messy to handle and does not set so it is difficult to remove any mistakes and will smudge if touched or brushed. Pigments and oxides can be added to the mixture to trail coloured lines but if the line is too thick, during the firing when the wax melts prior to burning away, the enclosed colour can bleed or run on vertical surfaces. Of course, this can be explored as a feature.

Adding pigments

Pigments added to hot wax can be used to great advantage in conjunction with other glazes/slips/stains and can be applied in all the usual ways. The more pigment that is added, the stiffer and therefore less fluid will be the mixture. However, a small amount of extra kerosine will give it back its flow. This in turn will make the mixture softer, so greater care must be exercised when handling. Also, there is a point where too much oxide and oil will render the wax unusable. Stronger oxides such as copper or cobalt work best because, since only a little is needed to give a strong colour, the flow of the wax is least impaired.

When applying hot wax to purely block out an area, the thickness of the layer is not too important as long as the whole area is covered. This is not so if pigments have been added to the wax. Any variation in thickness will mean greater or lesser concentrations of colouring pigment so all brush marks will show. A simple experiment to try is to dip your finger in pigmented wax (make sure that it is not so hot that it burns you) and dab it on to the clay surface. It will be seen that the area of the finger that is last to make contact with the surface (at the centre) will have a thicker build up of wax. Also, around the edge where the finger impression squeezed out some wax is also thicker, like the eye on a peacock's feather. This image will fire with the graduated tones.

Using foam stamps, coarse brushes or any means that will lay down different thicknesses of pigmented wax can be used to great advantage to give tonal qualities within an area. Oxides, clay and glaze stains and enamels can all be used in the resist.

If flat, defined, pigmented areas are required, then a paper or tape stencil will have to be laid down to allow wide, sweeping, even brush strokes to fill in the area, then the mask will have to be removed to leave a flat wax area ready to resist the next layer to be applied.

Precautions with wax

Since water-based or hot waxes dry on the surface that they are applied to, it is difficult to rectify any mistakes. It is therefore important to plan your design carefully before committing yourself on a piece. For example, how big should a repeat pattern be to fit evenly around a piece?

If you have little experience in using waxes and resists, it is always best to play around on test tiles. These should be at least 150 mm (6 inches) square to allow an unrestricted approach. This will

'High Tea' by Royce McGlashen (NZ). Decoration created with hot wax and iron sulphate wash.

not only allow you to get the feel of the flow of the wax but also to test the thickness of subsequent applications of stains/slips/glazes. It is always a wise move even with some experience, to decorate a test tile before commencing work to loosen up and get the feel of the process to be used as well as to test that the wax is at the correct consistency.

If the wax has been painted onto greenware, it is possible to carefully scratch away any mistakes as long as they are small. Mistakes on bisque ware are much more difficult to remove and usually the only solution is to refire the piece in your next bisque firing or to fire the piece to 600°C to burn off the wax and then start again.

It is possible to use solvents such a methylated spirits to dissolve the wax but usually this becomes a messy process and it can leave residues of wax in the pores of the clay which will cause problems when applying subsequent layers. If you do decide to use solvents, be very careful not to use liquids such as white spirit which will leave a greasy residue which will in turn resist subsequent layers. Remember – solvents are highly inflammable and will soak into the bisque if used in quantity. Therefore, when cleaning a piece, leave it until all the solvent has evaporated before firing. Otherwise the fumes may ignite in the kiln and cause an explosion.

If mistakes are made when applying wax onto an unfired glazed surface, they are comparatively easy to rectify. Because the glazed surface is powdery, the mistake can be removed by using a sharp, pointed craft knife to carefully lift it off. You must be careful not to flake the glaze. If the wax layer is thin, use a scraping motion. Do not try to use a pencil eraser or your finger to dab off a mistake as you would with water-based waxes as hot oil waxes are too greasy.

The most common problem with wax is runs caused by either an overloaded brush or by pressing too hard, or a combination of both. Practising on a test piece will allow you to gauge what is best.

Because the wax always retains some stickiness, once a piece has been decorated, you should not touch the pattern as it can be damaged. It is best to stand the piece on something like a tile or a bat whilst you are decorating it. This will allow easy movement around the studio. Once the piece has been finished prior to firing, it can be carefully picked up, for example to clean glaze runs off the base, as long as the damage

to the wax is no longer important. This is also true with water-based wax.

Since hot wax mixtures are continually heated during use, there is a constant evaporation of the paraffin/kerosine. It is therefore necessary to add more paraffin/kerosine during the long periods of use to keep a consistent mixture. The fumes that are given off are dangerous and so adequate ventilation is required. A removable flue can be easily constructed to join an extraction fan in the wall or ceiling. It is possible to buy a bayonet-fitting flue pipe so that the apparatus can be removed when not in use. Collapsible concertina flues are also available which look like a loosely wound wire spring with a canvas or plastic covering which, when not in use, concertina into a very small space. They are similar to those used with domestic tumble driers, but larger.

Brushes used in hot wax do not need to be cleaned after use. They can be smoothed into their natural shape and allowed to cool. They will come back to life when next heated. Standing the brushes in the hot mixture for long periods of time does shorten their life considerably. To avoid this, place a piece of thick wire across the top of the wax container to act as a brush rest. The heat from the wax below will keep them soft, ready for use but not hot enough to damage them.

Application over unfired glazes

Wax is most commonly used over unfired glazes for the subsequent application of further glazes or pigments. The marks made should look like a thin layer of varnish, or thicker depending upon the mixture or dilution. If the unfired glaze layer has been allowed to dry too much before waxing, it may lift off or cause crawling during firing. Softer wax mixes can alleviate this but it is better to decorate directly after glazing as long as the glaze has appeared to dry but still retains some moisture.

It should also be remembered that if a first glaze application has dried too much, any subsequent dipping/pouring/brushing of glaze will cause the layer below to bubble and lift from the bisque because of the passage of water through the base glaze layer. This will cause crawling when it is fired. A little dampness is always best. Cold working conditions can also cause hot wax itself to lift. This occurs when cold bisque ware is dipped into cold glaze and the warm wax, meeting the cold surface, chills too quickly so that the wax has no time to be absorbed slightly into the glaze layer, giving good adhesion. In very cold conditions in winter, it can be advantageous, although tedious, to warm the bisque or remove the water from the settled glaze bucket and replace it with hot water. Any wax application except very soft mix hot waxes will peel if left for long periods once applied.

When using hot wax, always be careful about burns.

Waxes once fired can leave a residue, particularly at lower temperatures, so the work may need to be brushed or sanded to remove this.

If large areas of wax are used on a piece, it must be remembered that it will take much longer to dry than a similar piece without wax. This is due to the waterproofing properties of wax. It is particularly important to be aware of this with unfired clay, because it might well explode in the kiln otherwise. Slab builders sometimes coat their joins in wax to help them dry more slowly thus preventing cracking.

Using glazes with wax

Patterns, shapes and marks can be made with waxes as described previously. However, if large panels of colour are needed or you have a piece that is too large to dip in one go, wax can be very useful.

Example 1 Panel of different colour

You wish to glaze a bowl in two coloured glazes, one colour being a large square in the middle. First dip the plate vertically four times to leave a bare bisque square in the centre. When the shine has gone off the glaze, the squared rim can now be waxed with either wax emulsion or hot wax. If you find it difficult to achieve an accurate square then first glaze oversize, wax to correct dimensions then scrape and sponge away to the wax edge. The second glaze can now be poured over the centre and out again without damaging glaze 1, thereby forming the central square.

Example 2 Glazing a large pot

We have all made something of a large scale only to find that it is too awkward to glaze in one go, our glaze bucket is too small to dip it fully, we don't have enough glaze depth and are in a hurry or we have no spraying equipment.

Mix the glaze and dip the vessel to the halfway point. When the shine has gone off, wax a wide band on the glaze to within 2 mm ($\frac{1}{16}$ inch) of the edge. Invert the vessel and dip the second half; the glaze flows off the waxed area resulting in an even all over coat.

Example 3 Different colours

The same method can be used as in example 2 but the second dipping can be a different glaze or the vessel can be dipped at both ends but not meeting in the middle. The glazed areas can be waxed and then dipped in another glaze to form a contrasting central band.

These are very simple examples and with a little imagination the reader can develop many more sophisticated results.

'Spontaneous Combustion' by Jeff Irwin (USA), 22 inch diameter. Decorated using black and white engobe and oil-based wax.

Jeff Irwin (USA)

Jeff Irwin's work utilises the qualities of oil-based waxes that have a better resisting capability when used with water-based colours, particularly when thin.

His early work used the wax in conjunction with coloured commercial underglazes creating abstract designs

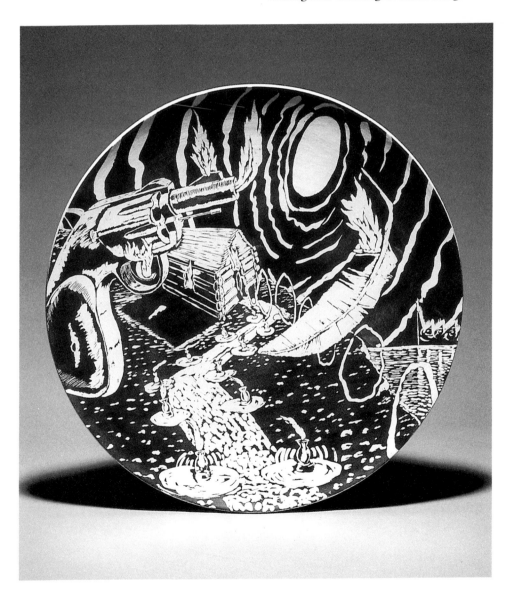

with hard edges. First, he would paint layers of colour on bone dry bisque ware, one thin coat for a transparent look or two thick coats for an opaque look. Mobile Brand room temperature oil-based wax was then painted onto the areas to be masked where the ground colour was to show through.

Another underglaze colour was painted carefully over the surface following the edge of the wax design and allowing the colour to just flow over the edge of the wax but not go all over it. The oil in the wax would cause the water-based colour to roll back to the edge of the wax, giving a hard edge with a greater build up of colour. If the colour is too thick or too much of the wax is covered, it will not be pushed back sufficiently to give a hard edge.

Because the wax has been placed over one layer of colour, it does not stick so well and with skill and care can be peeled off for further waxing and different colour application. More wax can be applied and other colours, building up as many layers and colours as needed, or the wax can be carved through before the next application. At this point the piece can be bisque fired but will come from the kiln with a residue of burnt wax, which must be washed off before applying a clear glaze and refiring.

This earlier method of working was mostly applied to functional platters but he is now producing more narrative, sculptural work which does not lend itself to the use of shiny, commercial glazes. Vitreous engobes are therefore used to give more of a satin sheen.

The work, heavily influenced by the qualities of wood block prints and Chinese stone rubbings, still requires that hard crisp edge. The pieces made in a variety of handbuilding techniques are left to completely dry and are then covered in two layers of white vitreous engobe and left to dry again. A drawing taken from carefully prepared sketches is done in soft pencil on the piece (this will burn away in the firing) to show the areas to be waxed.

The wax is then applied and two layers of black engobe are put on as described above. The design can be further altered with sgraffito and the lines filled with engobe. The base of the piece is then cleaned and given its once firing to cone 03.

The only problem encountered with this technique is that sometimes the engobe can pinhole during firing if the piece was not made smooth in the beginning. This can be avoided by lightly sponging the surface before decoration begins.

Chapter Four
Latex Wax or Latex Rubber Solutions

Latex 'waxes' are materials that come as natural latex emulsions or are produced by dissolving latex rubber in spirit-based solvents. They are not really waxes at all but they are often referred to as such. The spirit-based latexes tend to be quite liquidy and yellow or brown in colour whereas the latex emulsion is white and fairly viscous though still liquid.

These resists are sold by all ceramic suppliers but they can also be bought as watercolour painter's masking fluid and as a general purpose paper adhesive called 'Copydex'. They both come in an emulsion form. (See also the chapters on acid etching and grit blasting.)

The latex 'waxes' can be applied with a brush in much the same way as other waxes but they have the distinct advantage that when they have dried or the solvent has evaporated, you are left with a thin layer of rubber. This layer can be very easy to remove from dry glazed surfaces and green ware though on bisque ware it is more tempermental if the surface is not very smooth. This ability to remove the latex means that mistakes can be rectified easily and much more importantly, that a layer can be applied, coated over, the wax peeled away, another pattern painted on, coated over and the wax peeled away ad infinitum. In this way multi-layers of patterns can be laid down using different colours for different effects.

Another advantage of these resists is that because the water and the solvent

evaporate easily, they are ideal for wet or very damp surfaces as the solvent will evaporate and give a good resist. This is something that you cannot do with water-based waxes very effectively.

The disadvantage with the latex waxes is that brushes tend to become clogged and even though they can be cleaned they have a habit of losing their points and will not paint fine lines. The water-based latexes will clean off the brushes easily as long as they have not dried but the spirit-based ones are more of a problem. I could not find a supplier who could recommend a suitable solvent. The solution seems to be to allow the latex to dry and then wash the brushes in hot soapy water. Even so, the life of a brush can be quite short.

Application

Aside from brushes, resist trailers are also a useful way of applying the latex. These can be made from tubes of latex emulsion (Copydex being the easiest to obtain in the UK). The potter John Wheeldon has developed just such an instrument which is a very useful tool for drawing lines for his lustre work. The procedure is to remove the cap from a Copydex tube and drill a hole in the end of the cap. Glue into this cap (with a strong glue), the tip of a fine line fibre tip pen with the fibre removed. Then screw the cap back on to the tube. When the tube is squeezed, a thin continuous line

Lustre vessels by John Wheeldon (UK). Lines created with Copydex latex trailer.

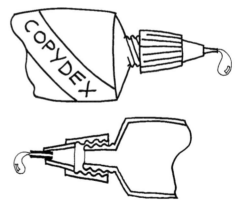

Right
Latex trailer using Copydex glue. The tube cap is drilled out and replaced with the tip of an old fine line fibre pen with the fibre removed. Very fine lines can be drawn with this clever versatile tool.

of latex will emerge which can be used for drawing on the work. When the tube is empty, it is a simple matter of removing the cap and screwing it on another tube. Soon you will have several spare caps as you empty the tubes and these can be set with different sized nozzles. Any latex that clogs the nozzle is easy to pull away before starting work. It is also helpful that the glue does not dry out in the tube. This is because when you stop squeezing, the trail stops and no air is sucked back into the nozzle.

Emulsion latexes can be diluted with water and used to lay down thin washes of resist that can hold colour on their surfaces as a thin sheen so enabling transparent washes of colour to be

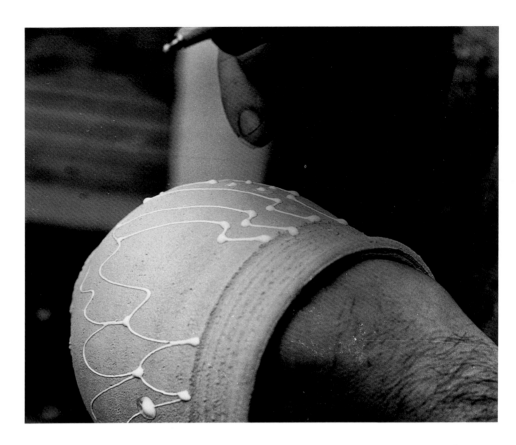

John Wheeldon trailing Copydex from the tube onto a pot.

achieved. If the colour is very dilute, it will pool in the areas of least resist giving a marbling effect.

I would not recommend applying latexes with sponges because the sponges cannot be cleaned successfully and they have a very short life.

Removal of the latex

A pair of tweezers is an ideal tool for starting to lift off the design. This can then be continued with the fingers. Peeling off the wax is like peeling off a series of rubberbands. If the design is complex and joins at some point, once the removal has started, the whole

design will come away as a stretchy rubber mesh. You must just keep gently pulling and turning the work until the resist finally flicks away from the surface. If, on the other hand, you are trying to remove a mistake, you must be careful that you don't end up removing all of the latex. Latex does not like to break; instead it tends to keep stretching which could lead to the whole rubber matting coming away. In these cases, it is best to pull away the rubber to the end of the mistake and then, using small, very sharp scissors, snip it away.

If latex is being used on a dry glazed surface or the subsequent layers are dry, it is inevitable that dust will be produced when the rubber is pulled away. Therefore, suitable precautions must be taken. This dust will either be from

deposits left on the latex or traces of material that has stuck underneath the latex. This can be both a health hazard and a nuisance in that the rubber may flick larger particles of glaze onto other areas of the work, thereby contaminating it.

Uses

Since latex glue is thicker than the latex produced for normal ceramic applications, the lines applied are quite proud of the surface. This can be exploited in a similar way to the tube lining which was used extensively in late 19th and early 20th century tile manufacture where thin walls of slip were trailed as the outline of a drawing and within these walls glazes could be flooded to give rich depths of glaze. This approach can be used with latex but with the added advantage that the latex can be pulled away leaving a groove in

Latex being removed showing its rubbery-ness and stretch. *Photograph courtesy of Hanna Lore Hombordy (USA).*

the areas of slip or glaze; these areas can be waxed with any wax and another application of glaze or slip applied to fill these grooves and thereby give your drawing an outline of a different colour.

It is not possible to paint on an area of latex wax and to sgraffito draw through it for fine details as the latex is too rubbery and it will peel away and drag instead of neatly cutting.

The technique of sponging green ware that has been shellacked or waxed to remove clay from the non-waxed areas to give different levels, also does not work well with latex. The latex tends to peel off during the sponging, destroying the crisp image.

Latexes are very versatile and the only serious disadvantage is the difficulty of cleaning tools. One artist who uses latexes is Carolyn Genders.

Carolyn Genders (UK)

Carolyn Genders is well-known in Europe for her use of wax and vitrified coloured slips built up in many layers to give textured interest and depth of colour. Carolyn's vessels are made in white-firing earthenware mostly by coiling, the initial surface being cleaned and scraped to give a smooth ground for decoration. Her vessels are simple, strong forms allowing the freedom of the decoration to excite the surface.

Most of her decoration takes place before the pot is bisque-fired, when it is completely dry. This gives more interesting lines and marks. Initially a layer of slip in one or more colours is sponged on all over to give a coloured ground. The sponges used are natural sponges and random-shaped pieces of foam that give a layer without an obvious pattern. Then free brush strokes are made in latex wax to begin to define a pattern. The wax dries immediately on application allowing quick, free, spontaneous marks.

Then more slip of other colours is either brushed over or applied with sponges, being dabbed or wiped across the surface. This can continue for several layers until a suitable complexity of colour is achieved. A light touch is essential. The slips should be the consistency of ordinary yoghurt, though thicker for sponging. Thin slips are more transparent and look more like watercolour paint. Carolyn spends a lot of time, when not potting, painting in both watercolour and oils and the dexterity of mark making in these media is a great influence when working on ceramics, the approach being intuitive rather than scientific. She believes in seeing what will happen although alongside this she is always testing. An alive feeling rather than a technique-led quality is essential for her work.

She then scratches at the surface cutting through the layers and into the body of the vessel. Soft coloured clays are gently pushed and burnished into these surface marks to make sure there is good adhesion between the dry clay body and soft clay. These areas can be carefully scraped with steel kidneys to remove excess clay, revealing the shape of the scratches and also to go back though the layers of overall slips to alter their appearance to a scraped look. The wax is applied with either nylon brushes or can be poured to give a linear pattern. She uses a selection of fan-shaped brushes which give very versatile marks. Sheep-haired chinese and nylon brushes work best for her as bristle and other hairs wear out and clog too quickly. If she requires very clean, geometric lines, Copydex is used, mixed with a little water to make it flow better. She also uses a mixture of petroleum jelly and candle wax mixed together hot for fine lines but this is not useful for large areas as it tends to break if scratched over and the slips can bleed under it.

Because slips are quite viscous the wax does not always totally resist and this is a quality that Carolyn has exploited in her work. The thicker the slips, the less they can be resisted and it is possible to obtain thin translucent layers of slip to adhere to the wax. As layer upon layer is built up the contrast between thick opaque slip and the translucent layers gives a three-dimensional quality to the final effect.

Slip over wax after firing creates certain problems. It must be sanded off if too thick as flakes of slip can lift during the firing leaving sharp points. Sanding off is quite laborious. It is done after the final firing with a good quality grinding stone. If this sanding is attempted at the bisque stage before the slip has vitrified there is a danger of removing areas of the pattern still required. Carolyn uses vitrified slips that contain a small amount of flux which allows them to melt just enough to give them a slight sheen which means that they have a good quality on their own without the use of glaze, but glazes are sometimes used.

Although the stains used in the slips are usually of a similar colour to their finished appearance, once they have been mixed into their slip base they become a pale version of their final fired colour and only with experience can one gauge the intensity of the colour of the final result. This element of uncertainty is something that Carolyn enjoys so the finished piece will always give surprises.

If a mistake is made while applying the slip it can be sponged off and new layers reapplied. After the desired result is achieved, the piece is bisque fired to 1000°C if it is to have a final finish of a thin layer of semi-matt opaque glaze brushed over it. If not, the pieces are fired along with the glazed pieces to 1160°C. It is very important that the green ware is very dry before firing and that the initial stages are very slow up to 600°C to burn off the latex. Too fast a firing will result in the gases from the latex coming though the slip layers too quickly causing the slip to flake or lift off. If on completion the result is not acceptable, it is possible to apply more layers of latex and slip over the glazed surface and refire the piece.

'Aurora' by Carolyn Genders (UK), 180 mm high. Decorated using vitreous slips in layers with water-based and latex wax between the layers.

Chapter Five
Spraying – Ordinary and Airbrush

There are several ways to apply slip/glaze/colour onto ceramics. The simplest, with minimal equipment, are by brushing, dipping and pouring. Dipping and pouring are fine for large areas of colour and where glazes are used that will merge together in the firing, evening out any blemishes caused during application. Brush work can be used for wide areas of colour and also for fine detailed work. The problem with these methods is that in many cases the finished surface required needs to be very flat and even, which is difficult to achieve. The solution for achieving a flat, even colour or surface is to spray.

The principle of spraying is that compressed air is blown through the spraying tool in which there is a reservoir of the material to be laid down. As the air passes through the tool, it draws the material into its path and deposits it on to the object as a moving mist or spray. It is usual for the colour to be mixed with water for spraying but any liquid can be used. The thicker the liquid to be sprayed, the higher the air pressure that is required or the bigger the jet size (hole through which liquid is forced) needed.

Spray guns

You will soon become accustomed to the correct mix that is suitable for your work. Spray guns come in different sizes depending on the type of work they are required to do. For general purpose spraying i.e. to just lay down a coating of slip or glaze, then guns with a larger jet size and bigger liquid reservoir would be the choice. As the work becomes more precise as with the use of enamels, then smaller, finer guns should be used. Your supplier will give guidance. Altering the air pressure to increase or decrease the flow of material and the jet all have bearings on the finished result.

The compressor that provides the air for the spray must give adequate pressure to give a good spray. It is usual to buy the spray gun and compressor at the same time so that they are compatible; all companies sell kits. The compressors are electrically operated. It is always easier to turn the pressure down on a compressor than to find that it is not powerful enough for the job. A pressure of about 30 pounds per square inch (psi) is usual for most jobs but the compressor should be capable of higher pressures. Compressors for use with the airbrush need not be so powerful. I would look for a compressor that would give up to 100 psi as a tool for all occasions. Always go for a portable compressor that is easy to move around for convenience.

Some compressors and electric spray guns (guns that have a small compressor within them, for domestic paint spraying) produce their air in rhythmic spurts as they pump. This in turn makes the spray come in spurts. This is more noticeable in some compressors than others. It is not a problem if it's for general spraying of glaze or slip but if the object of the exercise is to lay down fine, flat colour, the result of uneven spraying will be noticeable. The solution is always to buy a compressor with some kind of reservoir no matter how small. As the purchase of a compressor tends to be a 'once in a lifetime' event and as the work you may be doing in five years time may be very different, I would recommend buying the best you can to cover the widest range of uses.

Spray guns can be utilised with masks and resists to lay down broad areas of flat colour in one or multiple layers with the masks being removed at the required stages. The types of masks and resists are the same as those mentioned in other sections of this book and can be as simple or intricate as you wish them to be. Having said this, masks and resists that cannot be removed after spraying e.g. wax, do have disadvantages.

The spray that comes from the spray gun is made up of tiny droplets. As it moves through the air at speed, it may begin to dry. This happens most often when the material being sprayed is thick, as with glazes and slips, or if the spray gun is held far away from the work. As each tiny droplet reaches its destination,

Various sizes of spray gun, the smallest being for enamels and pigments, the middle for general purpose work and the largest for large areas of glaze or slip. Airbrushes for the finest work are very much smaller. *Courtesy of T.C.A.S. Spray Equipment (UK).*

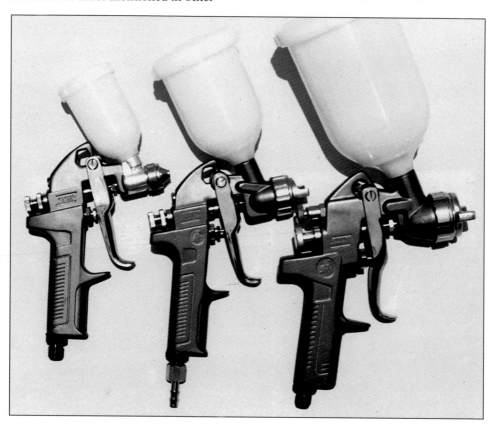

these droplets with them. Care must be taken when removing masks that the small particles of dry material do not fall onto other parts of the work and contaminate finished areas. In my own work I have used to advantage spray partially adhering to the wax to texture my decoration so that it is not so defined, thus giving more interesting colour variations.

The further away the object is from the spray gun the more powdery will be the sprayed surface. This powdery surface is easily damaged when touched as pressure will push the surface flat. So, if desired as a feature, the piece must not be handled after spraying. This is particularly a problem with slips or dry glazes.

If too much water is mixed with the material being sprayed, the object may not be able to absorb it quickly enough

A typical spray booth using a water tank to catch excess spray, essential for safe spraying. *Courtesy of T.C.A.S. Spray Equipment (UK).*

the object being sprayed, if porous, quickly sucks out the remaining moisture and this can leave the surface looking powdery and textured. For a glaze that will melt this is fine but with slips this rough surface will remain after firing. When using waxes, these dry droplets will not run off the wax and will tend to build up and then have to be removed with a sponge or wet brush.

Masks that can be removed will take

A typical small compressor suitable for all ceramic needs. *Courtesy of T.C.A.S. Spray Equipment (UK).*

and runs will develop. If a very liquid spray is required, it must be sprayed in thin, even coats leaving time for the previous coat to adhere. When spraying surfaces that are non-porous, great care must be taken to prevent build up of liquid that will begin to run. Again, several thin coats will be needed, drying only to dampness between each. If the coats are allowed to dry completely, the moisture from the next one will cause the previous ones to lift and crawl in the firing. Sticky spraying mediums and gums can be used to give coatings that dry hard or are very viscous and don't run, i.e. gum arabic, CMC or transfer enamel mediums.

When spraying flat colour, it is important that the spray is allowed to pass off the edge of the object before returning across it, otherwise at the point of direction change a thicker build up of colour will take place as the spray is momentarily stationary as it returns. Materials that tend to settle quickly in water like glaze stains or glazes containing a lot of frit must have suspenders added, otherwise if spraying is not quick the spray's constituents will alter as the work progresses. Various suspenders are available such as calcium chloride, bentonite and CMC. Only a small amount dissolved in water need be added for most situations. Many bought colours, particularly enamels, come suspended and ready to use. There are ranges of very interesting colours available for spraying that are mixed to iron out nearly all of the problems that can occur. Their manufacturers' addresses are listed at the rear of the book.

Techniques and problems with spraying are similar for all types of work and are covered below in the airbrush section.

Airbrush

If very fine work is involved particularly with the use of coloured stains, the tool for the job is the airbrush. The airbrush works on the same principle as the spray gun in so much as the flow of compressed air propels the ceramic material out of the nozzle as a spray. The difference is that the airbrush is capable of giving the finest and most delicate application of colour. We have all seen the car drawings, record covers and technical illustrations that are so realistic but have been painted with the airbrush. Such control and fineness of detail is also perfectly possible when using ceramic materials with the airbrush.

The instrument itself is quite simple and many companies like Amaco in the US supply a whole range of colours specifically designed for airbrush use. The restriction of the possibilities is in the user because the airbrush requires meticulous preparation of masks and design to achieve the most detailed of results. Having said this, if you require fine detail with subtleties of shading but not so a soup can looks *exactly* like a soup can, the airbrush is for you. But if you want the soup can to look exactly like a soup can in ceramic, it can be achieved but only with the airbrush.

The basic principles of successful airbrushing are careful preparation of the masks to be used taken from accurate drawings, careful preparation of the colours to be sprayed and meticulous cleanliness as mistakes on fine work are difficult to rectify.

First the design: A working drawing must be produced that is the size of the piece to be sprayed either in full colour for the inexperienced or in black and white. From this the masks will be produced. The masks can be of any material that can be laid close to the surface of the work but thin clear plastic sheet is commonly used. This material is called 'frisket'. Frisket can be either adhesive on one side to stick to the work or not. It must be remembered that if it does stick to an area that has been already sprayed, there is a danger of the glue removing or damaging the surface. Therefore, non-adhesive masks are preferable. Firing between colours will alleviate this problem but it does make the work drawn out and disjointed.

When the mask is laid on the object, if it does not make good contact at the edges, the fine spray will creep under the edge giving a fuzzy line. This condition can be used to great effect as well as being a fault. The image can be given a misty quality and create a feeling of depth to the flat image. Found natural objects such as leaves can be laid onto the work with excellent results where underspray is used to highlight the curls at the edge. The American potter Hanna Lore Hombordy uses all these techniques with great skill.

Any object that is used, if light, must be weighted down, otherwise the air from the nozzle will either move it or blow it off the piece during spraying. Artists I have talked to use a whole variety of weights from small tin cans, nuts, washers, small heavy objects and pieces of soft clay. A stencil can be held down with the finger or stuck down if there is no colour layer below to be damaged. Handheld stencils do have the disadvantage that you are then working one handed so everything must go correctly first time.

Although an image may have a strongly defined outline, the beauty of the airbrush is that it can be used free hand in a similar way to the graffiti drawings that are common these days. By adjusting its distance from the surface, the airbrush can give broad sweeps of colour down to fine detail. In fact, when first using an airbrush, executing some free hand work is a good way of getting the feel of the tool.

The angle of the spray in relation to the surface of the piece greatly affects the quality of the finished result. The airbrush spray can be likened to the rays of the sun and the shadows that they cast. If the airbrush is held at 90° to the surface of the work, the result will be a disc of colour very dense in the middle with a thinner, fuzzy edge. The further from the surface it is held, the bigger the disc, the less dense the colour and the fuzzier the edge; the closer, the smaller and denser the disc. If the airbrush is tilted from the surface, the more oval and elongated is the spray pattern with the nearest area being densest through to only a trace of colour at the far edge. This quality of spray is ideal for shading an image to make it look three-dimensional. The angle it is held at and the distance away is therefore altered during the execution of an image to graduate the colour density as required.

When first using an airbrush, simple exercises can be undertaken like cutting a disc, triangle and rectangle from a mask and practising spraying them to look like a sphere, a cone and a tube. These exercises can be done with ink on paper before experimenting and wasting expensive ceramic colours.

For very complicated work, the best surface to work on is one as flat as possible but, although curved areas are more difficult, careful planning does give good results. When laying a flat mask on a curved surface, it will tend to crinkle at the edges. So, small darts need to be cut to allow the mask to curve around the

A simple stencil cut from upholstering plastic held down with washers.

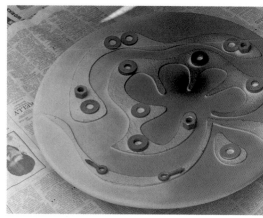

The plate is sprayed.

The mask is removed to reveal the image.

Hand shading is done with an airbrush.

Natural objects are held in place for spraying.

Complex shapes are held in place with weights.

The sprayed plate.

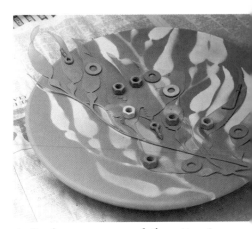

As the shapes are removed, the pattern is revealed. *All photographs courtesy of Hanna Lore Hombordy (USA).*

'Spring Night' by Hanna Lore Hombordy (USA), 17 inch diameter. Airbrushed design using paper shapes.

object and still remain flat on the surface thus avoiding the spray creeping under the mask.

Thin clay sheets cut to shape can be laid on the work with care or latex wax can be used which is peeled away afterwards. A positive or a negative image is achieved by either using a shape cut from a sheet and sprayed through or the cut out piece can be sprayed around. The spraying can be as flat colour or graduated colour as desired.

Two or more colours can be used laid down one over the other. Of course, one colour over another may affect each to some extent and this can pose problems but it can also be used to advantage. However, if it is a problem, there are a range of opaque colours available that do not have this problem. Light colours can be laid over dark ones completely blocking out the colours below. The development of these types of colour now means that any image is possible no matter how detailed. Product details are at the back of the book.

We have talked about simple renderings with the airbrush either used free hand or from drawings and I would suggest that is the place to start before tackling more complicated work. But it

Simple exercises using cut out shapes like circles and cones to play with to create a three-dimensional image.

must be said that the range and interest in the work is easy to accomplish with the most simple of masks and a variety of colours.

For very realistic images much more preparation is required. The image to be produced must first be rendered on paper – as before in either black and white or colour. Colour is better as one can more easily differentiate between one area and another, especially if complicated shading is to be used. The final working drawing must be the same size as the final image as this will be used to cut the masks. Reduced or enlarged photocopies are very useful to reduce unnecessary drawing. The object the image is to be applied to can be green ware, bisque or glazed. Choose the material you find best for the mask – either papers or plastic. Clear plastic frisket is better as not only can you see though it to help positioning on the work but it can be washed and re-used again and again.

Lay the frisket on the drawing and fix it firmly in place with tape. There is nothing worse than the sheet slipping while you are cutting. Then cut out the elements of the image with a sharp craft knife or scalpel. It is helpful to number them and lay them to one side on a photocopy of the image so that they don't become muddled up. Keeping the break down of the image to simple shapes is the easiest way to work and shading can be done within this area free hand. Several sheets of plastic will need to be cut, each one having the negative image (the hole) of the shapes of that colour to be cut from it. If it is a very curved shape, then several overlapping pieces may be needed to follow the contours, with or without darts to help. It is most important that a generous border is left around the negative image to prevent overspray contaminating already rendered areas. It is most sensible to start at the background of the image and cut the frisket working forward to the front or top of the image i.e. the last and smaller areas to be sprayed. They can be numbered for order of use.

The object to be sprayed must be clean, dust and oil free, otherwise there will be delamination of the slips, underglazes and glaze applied. The first mask can be positioned and spraying commence. The preparation of the colour is very important as is the condition of the airbrush. The colours must be very fine in particle size and of a very smooth consistency. Commercially-bought colours specifically for airbrush use will be ready to use once mixed thoroughly and can be diluted to taste. Always dilute with distilled water as tap water can contain impurities that cause the liquid to flocculate giving an uneven spray. Companies that specialise in ceramic colours for airbrushing supply special thinning liquids. Colours or oxides not designed specifically for an airbrush should be sieved at least through a 200s mesh sieve and if possible, ball milled so that they are ultra fine. The colour should be the consistency of milk for spraying but each person will have his own preference. The liquid should have a binder added to prevent smudging previously coloured areas; CMC, a commercially-manufactured binder, is the preferred binder of many artists.

The spraying should not be done in one coat unless one thin rendering will be enough. The best way to achieve good depth and opaqueness of colour is by spraying three thin coats, leaving each one to dry before the next. This has two purposes: one, the frisket if plastic is used is not porous so the spray on it does not

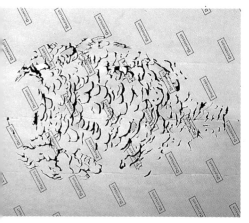

a.

b.

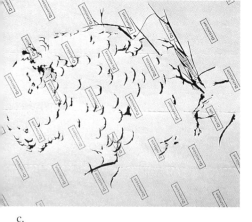

c.

d.

The stencils needed to reproduce a picture. a, b and c are drawings for stencils of different colours; d is the original artwork.

dry and if there is too much of a wet build up, the air from the airbrush can push this off the mask onto the object thereby spoiling the flat colour, and two, it can also prevent a build up or ridge at the boundary where the mask ends and the sprayed area begins. This is similar to the ridge that is found when applying slips and glazes in a more conventional masking. This in itself is not a problem but if another image is sprayed across this, the edge of the area below will show. It may also prove advantageous to remove the frisket and wash it before each spraying, drying it thoroughly before repositioning. Secondly, if a large area of colour is to be laid down,

spraying can be done across the work from a different direction, thereby increasing the chance of an even coat. Sometimes spraying in a circular motion helps too.

The coats should be allowed to dry thoroughly before positioning the next mask, to allow the binder to do its job. Areas that have been completed can also be waxed to protect them if there is a danger of overspray. Any overspray can be carefully removed with a sponge at the end. Each colour can then be laid down in turn with any shading necessary until the image is complete. It can then be left as it is and fired to have a matt surface or a glaze can be oversprayed if required.

The airbrush itself is a very delicate instrument and needs careful looking after if it is to give good service. Ceramic materials, unlike paints, are very abrasive and it will be found that after a time the nozzle and needle inside (which controls the spray flow) will become worn and will need to be replaced if a good delicate flow of colour is to be maintained. The airbrush must be washed through and cleaned thoroughly for each colour use and at the end of work not only to prevent cross contamination of colour but also to prevent any remaining colour from drying inside the tool and affecting the spray.

Airbrushes can be temperamental giving a splattering of colour or being blocked completely instead of giving the required fine spray. This is always due to badly prepared colour (not fine enough) or a badly maintained tool. The airbrush is not for the sloppy!

Faults

The main faults are as follows:

Spattering – liquid too thick or lumpy, pressure too low, needle worn or bent, tip worn or bent, erratic pressure from compressed air source, wrong head assembly.

Spidering – too close to surface being sprayed, liquid too thin, pressure too high or a combination of the above.

Unevenness – build up on tip and needle, liquid not homogeneous, erratic pressure source.

Burst of liquid – Build up on tip and needle.

Pattern too wide or coarse – worn tip.

No liquid sprayed – clogged reservoir or intake, liquid too thick, pressure too low, tip clogged.

Spray not centred – bent needle, unevenly worn tip, or both, dirty head assembly.

There are no books to my knowledge that deal with airbrush techniques for ceramic applications but there are several on the market for the use of paints and ink and the information they contain on maintenance and techniques are the same as for ceramic. *Air brush The Complete Studio Handbook* by Radu Vero (New York: Watson Guptill) is a very good book.

Experience is the best teacher so don't be discouraged!

Mike Head (UK)

The British artist and designer Mike Head specialises in producing large tile panels for public spaces, such as underground stations, using a fine spray gun to lay down colours. With such commissions the design is executed onto bought-in standard glazed vitreous tiles.

The design, once approved by the client, is drawn onto sheets of tracing paper full size. The tiles are laid on the bench in areas of about 6 m × 2 m, spaced as they will finally be mounted, including the grouting line. The bench is covered with a rubber sheet that keeps the tiles securely in the position where they are placed. The traced design is then transferred onto the tiles using graphite dust rubbed onto the reverse of the trace and the design being drawn around. The graphite burns away in the firing. Areas of about 1 metre (39 inches) square are worked on at a time. This represents the distance that it is comfortable to cover with the sweep of the arm that is spraying the colour.

The area to be sprayed is then covered with a sheet of self-adhesive film. There are various types available and they can be matt or shiny. The matt is better as the surface helps prevent runs developing from the film onto the tile during spraying. There are films which are temporary protective overlays or masking medium with a non-setting adhesive and types which have a setting adhesive which have other applications. Mike Head has found by experience that films with a setting adhesive work best but it does mean that all stencil cutting and spraying must take place within 24 hours so that the stencil can be removed before firing. After this time the adhesive will have cured and the film cannot be removed so the work is ruined.

Small air bubbles trapped between the film and the tile do not cause problems as any that cross a graphite line will be punctured when the design is cut out. The first cuts to be made are down the gaps between the tiles so that the film can be slightly wrapped around the edges. This will also enable the enamel colour to travel around the tile edge. The thin white line that would have been left around the edge of the tile had they been silk screened (where the taut screen cannot curve around the edge) would have been unslightly and ruined the overall effect, but with spraying this does not occur.

Taking a sharp knife areas of film are now cut away revealing the tile below. Only the areas of one colour are removed at a time. The cut edges are rubbed over with the finger to make sure there is good contact to prevent spray creep. The mask could have been cut and then applied to the tile but being plastic it stretches and the results are not as satisfactory. A strip of fully masked tiles from the metre square is placed on a board and can now be sprayed.

The enamels he uses have to be carefully prepared to give good even colour. If he is spraying onto an unglazed vitrified tile, a flux has to be added to the enamel, about 5 per cent in his case. He uses Blythes C4 flux. This makes the enamel more durable after firing. For the more usual glazed tiles, the enamel has a cold cure medium added which aids the stick and drying of the coating. Again Blythes 65/42 medium is used and 10 per cent is added. The powdered enamel and medium has tap water added until the consistency of single cream is reached. The liquid is ground in a mortar and pestle to dispel any lumps and ensure thorough mixing. This is then sieved through at least a 200s mesh sieve. It must be remembered that although enamels are ground very fine by the manufacturer, they still may contain the odd small lump. This can either block the spraying jet or cause a moment of splatter which can ruin an even surface. Therefore sieving is always done prior to working. An enamel mixture can be stored but if it is kept over 48 hours, it must be resieved as lumps will start to form in the liquid, due to flocculation caused by the tap water.

Mike sometimes warms the tiles to shorten the drying time of the enamels, but if they are too warm and dry too quickly, you will not get a clean crisp edge.

The strip of tiles is sprayed with four layers of colour and the spray is always taken beyond the end of the tiles to avoid the double thickness that occurs at the change of direction as you move back and forth. The first layer you can only just see. It is laid down in a vertical movement, the second in a horizontal movement and the two others follow the diagonals. This ensures a very even coating. As the enamel has the cold cure medium, it means that the spray layer can be allowed to be wet but not to puddle. The amount of wetness is more towards damp than shiny. This is difficult to describe and must be discovered by trial and error. If it is too wet after about a minute, the enamel will move away from the cut edge of the mask so giving a poor finish at this point. Mike sprays with the tile strip lying flat. The gun is between 200 mm and 250 mm (8–10 inches) from the tiles with a pressure of 15–20 psi. The gun is cleaned with water between colours.

After four coats a fan is used to speed the drying of colours at which point the mask can be removed and the colour fired. There is a difference between wet and dry and the mask has to be removed before the enamel is bone dry but after it is wet. The required damp state is one that experience will help you to recognise. If the enamel is too dry, the edge will crumble as the film is removed and if too wet, the enamel can move without the edge of the film to stop it. The enamel is not fixed in any way so if the surface is touched, it will be damaged. Because of this it is possible to scratch away the enamel. This is a technique which Mike uses to produce texture and shading.

The tiles are fired between each colour to 780°C to 810°C depending on the hardness of the tile glaze. The idea is to get the enamel to sink slightly into the glazed surface so as to appear more part of the glaze than on it. Unglazed vitrified tiles that are sprayed with the enamel and flux come out with a matt surface that is similar to the tile surface.

The tiles are then set up again and he repeats the process for each colour. With each subsequent colour the edge of the previous fired colour has a slight raised edge and this can be used to help guide the knife around the shapes so that the film is a tight fit giving colours that butt up well to each other. Handheld cardboard masks are used to give some spray shading.

Mike Head also uses silk screens for working directly onto the tiles or for screening transfers, usually lettering. The letters are formed on the screen with sellotape, then a blue masking medium is squeegeed over the screen blanking out the mesh. The sellotape is removed revealing the shapes ready to be screened.

The masking medium is air drying and after use can be removed with solvents so that the screen can be re-used.

Jeff Cole (USA)

Jeff first began making objects with painted images using slips, oxides, glazes and stains and he experimented with wax, latex wax, and paper. As his work developed the images became more and more detailed and complex with the surfaces acting like a canvas. Originally high-firing, it became apparent to him that to achieve bright complex images would need low temperature firing and the use of the airbrush. The majority of his images are produced with underglazes and freehand airbrushing and brush work accompanied by masking done with plastic frisket material. The use of paper, aluminium foil, loose fibres and found objects, architectural templates and various widths of masking and graphic art crepe tapes are also used.

Painting is done on both green ware and low-temperature bisque to provide as porous a surface as possible that will accept the wet airbrush medium rapidly. A clean dust- and oil-free surface on the clay is important to prevent delamination of the applied layers from the clay object. The mediums for spraying his images are meticulously prepared in the manner described in the airbrush section.

To paint his images with the airbrush, he begins with a finished line drawing of the image. This is done with a fine technical pen on white board or tracing paper mounted on white ridged board. By experience he has learned to break down complex shapes into simple basic ones. The background of the image is tackled first when preparing the friskets working forward to the top image. Once the images have been established the frisket cutting begins.

He uses a clear stable plastic acetate which is not affected by water. This is used in the printing industry for making composite negatives and can be bought in shops that supply silk screen and printing products. He always leaves a generous border of plastic around the cut shape to avoid overspray. A sheet of acetate is laid over the drawing and secured with tape, the shapes are cut out leaving negative areas. These shapes, centred on the piece of plastic, are used to block in the colours. The pieces are labelled with indelible pen to get registration correct and for future use.

When spraying, the frisket is held in place by hand or weighted in place with small heavy metal washers. Spraying is done in several thin coats wiping the frisket clean in between. Each coat is allowed to dry thoroughly before the next is applied and because he is using opaque colours, one colour can be used to cover another.

When finished, the pieces are bisque fired, glazed and fired to cone 04.

Nan S. Smith (USA)

Nan S. Smith makes very detailed sculptures and wall reliefs which are highly decorated with intricate realistic images airbrushed onto their surface. She has a strong interest in the spiritual existence 'within' which provides the impetus and the conceptual basis for the figurative sculptures, wall reliefs and installations; metaphors for aspects of the human condition. A sensibility for those things, not seen but felt, is at the core of the work. A conscious effort is made to synthesise visual information to create an unusual series of symbolic imagery. Realism is manipulated to create a sense of surprise. Unusual visual synthesis, strange juxtapositions: surreal, imaginary, and dreamlike, are a major part of the visual language of her work.

The pieces are constructed out of heavily grogged low-fired sculpture clay: a flesh coloured earthenware that matures at Cone 06–04. After construction they are bisque fired to Cone 09 in an electric kiln.

The colours that she uses are manufactured by the Duncan, Amaco and Reward colour companies. The colours are usually underglaze colours and can be used without glaze if a matt surface is required but she overglazes with thin matt glazes as this gives a better colour intensity. Shiny glazes are not used as the reflective quality will

Lidded boxes by Jeff Cole (USA), 19 inch diameters. Airbrush decoration.

distract from the complex forms. Commercially-produced colours are easier to work with as they stay in suspension better in the airbrush reservoir; extenders can be added to give a finer, more translucent coating. The pieces are dampened before applying colour by spraying water through the airbrush, as this enables better absorption of the colour application into the surface. Duncan Cover Coats are used to first spray flat colour fields and also to cover areas that have become muddy and ill-defined.

The resist materials that she most often uses are tapes of various widths, wax resist emulsion and self-sticking stencils. Masking tape and Formaline tapes stick easily to bisque ware. Tapes are used off the roll for grids and bands or hard rectangular edges. Wax emulsion is used to seal off areas once the colour and glaze have been applied. These areas are built up in stages and the wax protects the previously completed area from overspray and accidental touching.

Stencils are cut from self-sticking label paper with a peel away backing and comes in $8\frac{1}{2} \times 11$ inch (21.5×28 cm) sheets. Nan finds that the label paper is easier to cut than other products she has tried and because her images are very complex the stencils naturally become complex. They are cut out with scissors from carefully prepared drawings. Multi-coloured images are organised into colour separation in much the same way as a printmaker would plan a silk screen. Once all the stencils are cut and organised, the spraying can begin; any additional masks that may be required are cut as the work progresses.

The sculptures, reliefs and tile units are all airbrushed in an upright position. Figurative sculptures that are free-

'Illusions' by Nan S. Smith (USA), 32 inches high. Airbrushed and sprayed image.

standing are placed on a large turntable. Reliefs and tiles are propped vertically against a banding wheel, which has been padded with foam rubber, to elevate and secure the form. Surface information is laid on and built up in much the same way as a painting, colours being built up from light to dark. The pigments are diluted or extended with Duncan Thin 'n Shade to give the different transparencies of colour. The colour seen on the surface is much the same as the finished fired result and is normally applied in thin coats to build up to the intensity required. Large areas to be covered are sprayed in a circular motion which she finds gives a better even cover. Tape and paper towels are used to prevent overspray when doing large areas.

The stencils for the colour separation are notched so that accurate registration can be achieved. The stencils are placed against the surface as close as possible. On flat areas they are held by removing the adhesive backing and sticking the stencil in place and on compound curves they are held with tape. The paper stencils are blotted once the pigment has been sprayed to dry them which prolongs their life and prevents them curling. After the image has been laid down with spraying, further colour is applied by hand. Colour and tonal modulation is completed with the airbrush by manipulating a cardboard shield; one hand sprays while the other moves the shield.

Once all the pigment has been laid down glazes are applied by both spraying and with a brush which is well loaded with glaze to prevent the colour lifting onto the brush. A mixture of 1/3 glycerine to 2/3 water can be sprayed over the surface which acts as a fixative similar to that used on a charcoal drawing. Various glazes and frits are used to create the desired surface quality and the pieces are finally fired to between Cone 06–04.

'Guide' (detail) by Nan S. Smith (USA), 7 foot long. Airbrushed earthenware. *Photograph by Allen Cheuvront Studios.*

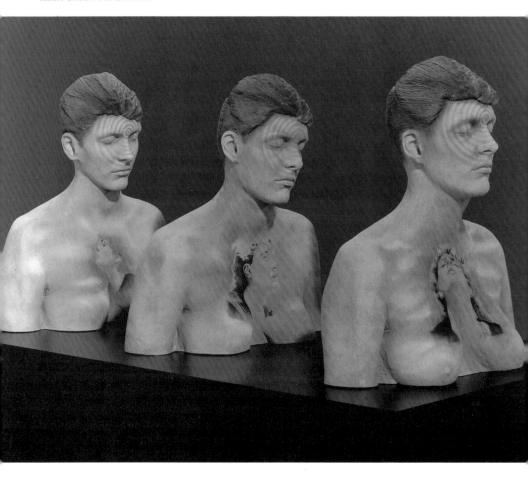

Douglas Kenny (USA)

Douglas Kenny makes large platters (up to 600 mm (24 inches) in diameter) which are jiggered onto plaster moulds after the surface has been extensively altered with texture and colour.

Large slabs about 10 mm ($\frac{3}{8}$ inch) thick are rolled out and the surface is smeared with manganese dioxide or black slip onto which are added subsequent layers of powdered clays from dark brown to white. Then commercial stains are added to areas and the whole slab is inverted. Sections are cut away into which are placed clay that has been textured by pressing onto cinder building blocks. The joints are sealed with coils to prevent cracking at later stages. The whole slab is now put through a slab roller and inverted onto a plaster mould centred on a wheel. The back is smoothed with a sponge, a foot ring is applied and the platter is left to stiffen. Once removed from the mould it is allowed to dry very slowly (for about three weeks) on its rim to prevent warping. It is then bisque fired. After bisque firing the piece is thoroughly washed to remove any dust that may prevent the adhesion of the underglaze colours and the masks, which will now be applied.

A design is roughed out in pencil and large areas are masked out with 50 mm (2 inches) wide masking tape which is wide enough to prevent overspray. The range of Duncan colours are used to spray within the masked areas. Douglas has tried other manufacturers but has found that the Duncan range with their cover coat does not lift off when subsequent layers of masking tape are applied. Once large areas are complete, smaller areas are decorated with latex wax that can be peeled off and small adhesive stickers that can be purchased at any stationery shop. Other geometric shapes needed are cut from masking tape.

In older work he employed the use of photo silk screens to airbrush through to give photographic images. The screens are removed from their frame so they can be moulded to the curve of the piece. They work best using the largest mesh screen and with images that have as much contrast as possible.

Old manila filing envelopes make good masks as they are slightly absorbent. They soak in the underglaze and can be used several times before becoming too wet. Plastic sheet stencils tend to get wet too quickly but they can be used over and over again. Plastic engineers' templates are also employed and found geometric objects, like the masking tape rolls, can be used for making rings. The problem with found objects is that they are generally not flexible enough so the spray tends to creep under the edges giving a fuzzy edge, but they are good as

'Plate Grid' by Douglas Kenny (USA), 21 inch diameter. Wax tapes and stencils with sprayed pigments. Earthenware. *Photograph by Eric Rippert.*

Detail of 'Plate #MC9' by Douglas Kenny (USA).

Finally a commercial clear glaze is applied but again some areas are masked off to give different surface textures after the final firing.

The completed plate is then fired very slowly because of its size to Cone 06. Once glaze fired, it is then rubbed with black indian ink to bring out some of the texture and crazing. Occasionally additions of gold leaf are added to give focal points in the work.

Douglas approaches his work like a painter to a canvas and the positioning of the geometry is very important and many hours are spent building up the complex layers to create the finished result. He also produces sculptural pieces that are treated in the same way but are saggar-fired with salts to give different final colours.

Sasha Wardell (UK/France)

Sasha Wardell slipcasts fine bone china forms. She then airbrushes geometric patterns of underglaze colours directly onto the previously high-fired pieces. She is influenced by illustrative painting, architectural elements, fabric design and artists like Elizabeth Fritsch, Jacqueline Poncelet and Eileen Nesbit in the ceramics world.

Once cast the forms are fired to 1000°C to harden them so that they can be sanded without breaking to obtain a very smooth finish. They are then fired again to 1260°C to vitrify them. Any area not to be sprayed is masked out with masking tape. The areas on which the decoration is to appear, are built up with torn random pieces of tape up to four layers deep. Alternatively, intricate patterns are cut directly from the tape on the surface. Because the work has been high-fired, the cutting of the tape directly on the surface does not give rise to any

a ground onto which more precise images can be laid with masking tape. Their advantage is that they are quick to use. On some plates he uses a fast mask spray technique by laying down two pieces of paper on top of one another at angles and then spraying. Then he moves them to a different area and sprays again repeating them all over the surface and changing colours as needed.

Once five or six layers of underglaze colour have been applied, other areas are masked with tape and a crawling glaze is applied with oxides and stains added.

damage even though they are extremely thin. The cut tape is used in conjunction with torn areas.

It is important that the tape should not get too hot i.e. applying it in the sun or in an over-warm studio, as this makes the glue softer and it can remain on the surface of the piece when the tape is peeled off. Masking and spraying takes place therefore on the same day and she keeps the masking tape in a fridge prior to use. Only a small number of pieces are decorated at any one time.

Spraying is done with a mixture of 1/3 colour to 2/3 glaze, all bought from commercial suppliers. Colours are intermixed to give different colours and mixed with white to give different

Slip cast vessels by Sasha Wardell (UK/France). Airbrushed patterns using layers of masking tape and matt coloured glazes.

shades. These are then ground in a pestle and mortar for about 10 minutes and then sieved through a 200s mesh sieve two or three times as a smooth consistency is essential for smooth spraying

It is most important when using an airbrush that the spraying medium is correctly prepared if good quality results are to be obtained. An airbrush is a very temperamental instrument if this is not done.

Since her work is vitrified before the colour is applied, it is important that the mixture is not too thin as it will run off the piece as no water is absorbed into the clay. If it is too thick, the airbrush will clog or splutter. Because ceramic materials are very abrasive, it is essential to carefully clean and check the airbrush and replace nozzles and needles when they become worn.

The colours are then applied in a specific order starting with the background colour which is usually the darkest; then a layer of masks is removed. Subsequent colours are then applied removing a layer of masks for each one until the final design is achieved. Although the colour sprayed will go over the previous one, knowing by experience what colour changes will take place does not make this a problem and, for example, if green was required then yellow would be used over blue. Care is taken never to touch the decoration as it is easily damaged. There is no firing between colours.

Once all the masks have been removed, the areas without colour are carefully cleaned with acetone to remove any glue residues to which particles of colour can stick. Also, the glue itself can leave a mark thus contaminating the finished result. Cotton buds are used for this careful process so as not to disturb the colour. Some pieces have the sprayed surface partially washed off after application to give a marbled effect. This was discovered by accident when washing off some colour that had gone wrong. The effect is difficult to control and depends on the flow of water, slow running is best. Once complete they are fired to 1120°C and polished with fine wet and dry abrasive paper to give them a smooth sheen.

Sasha Wardell cutting masking tape to shape on a piece prior to spraying. *Photograph by Nicole Creston.*

Below
Tea set by Sasha Wardell (UK/France). Airbrushed patterns using layers of masking tape and matt coloured glazes. *Photograph by Nicole Creston.*

Chapter Six
Paper and Adhesive Tapes, Papers and Films

Although all masking and resisting materials can be used in all processes and stages of the clay object, some are more suitable than others, and there are always exceptions to rules. Generally though, if the area to be covered is large then it is best to use papers, tapes and films instead of water-based waxes and latexes which are more expensive. Also, masks made of papers, tapes and films can be pre-cut or cut to shape when in position. This makes them a versatile tool when marking and resisting.

Paper

I will define paper as a non-plastic material that is bought usually in sheets and is non-adhesive in its natural state. There are paper tapes that can be bought with an adhesive backing but I shall deal with them in the section on Tapes.

Paper is an ideal material for masking as it is so versatile in that it can be cut or torn into an unlimited variety of shapes. All papers are worth experimenting with. However, an ability to absorb water makes the paper more useful when resisting as the damp paper sticks to surfaces more easily. The less absorption, the less use the paper is. In the damp state, it will also bend and contour itself better to a curved surface.

The layer to be applied over the paper mask has a bearing on the choice of paper, as the thicker the layer, the thicker should be the paper so that it has enough strength to be removed without tearing. The longer the layer is left, the harder it will become as water is absorbed from it and therefore the more difficult it will be to remove the paper. It must also be remembered that damp paper has less strength than in the dry state. A balance therefore has to be struck between strength when wet and time to execute the masking process.

Newspaper is always a good starting point as it is readily available, easy to cut and shapes well when damp. It must be remembered that newspaper has a grain and when cutting fine strips these must be done along the grain. Otherwise they will tear easily when being handled, especially once the layer to be resisted has been applied. It is easy to find the grain direction by tearing a sheet of newspaper, it will tear easily in a straight line in the grain direction. The other way the tear veers off and cannot be controlled. Newsprint is easy to obtain blank from good art material suppliers if detailed designs need to be drawn out that may be visually interfered with by printing. If long strips are needed, tape the sheet at the edges to a board and cut with a knife and ruler.

The most versatile paper to use is one that is matt on one side and glossy on the other. The type used in florist and butcher shops comes into this category. Its versatility is in the fact that the matt side allows the paper to be dampened to stick to the object while the shiny side

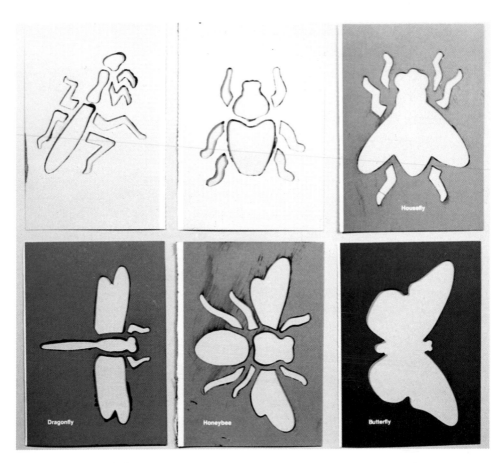

Bought paper stencils that come in books
ready to use, in various subjects.

Right
The image produced.

gives it strength. Being thicker than
newspaper, it does not mould itself to
contours so well and for more
complicated undulations, darts need to
be cut to remove crinkles, in much the
same way as clothes patterns have darts
to shape a garment. It is applied to the
object matt side down.

Torn paper has a very pleasing ragged
edge that is reproduced well when used
as a mask.

If the layer being applied over a paper
mask is very thick, it can cover the
surface in such a way that it cannot be
seen where the mask has been laid. This
is particularly true with newsprint as the
moisture in the slip/glaze is absorbed

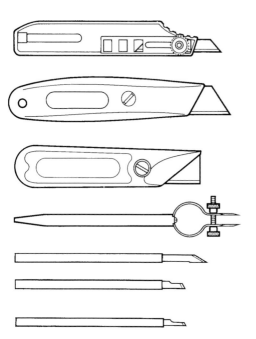

Various knives suitable for cutting masks including the 'Griffhold Dual Cutter' (fourth down). *Courtesy of Griffin Manufacturing Co., Inc. (USA).*

equally as well through the paper and the clay as the unmasked clay areas. As it is thin, a ridge of an outline is not always apparent. Shiny sided papers are less absorbent so there is no build up of layer and therefore they always show as a depression which makes them easy to locate and remove. If used with care, these types of paper can be washed and used more than once.

Papers are useful on unfired clay in all stages of dampness and on bisque ware in damp or matt surfaces situations such as when slips are employed with these masks. With bisque ware it must be realised that as the bisque absorbs the water from the paper, it will begin to lose its 'stick' and start to peel and curl away from the surface. Therefore, it is important to dampen the bisque just enough for the paper to stay put and the next layer to stiffen up and not run. Simple, bold designs work best. Adhesive tapes are often a better solution on bisque ware. Dusty surfaces can give problems with the 'stick' of a mask so wax may be a better solution. When working on flat surfaces e.g. in the bottom of dishes, it may not be necessary to dampen the paper at all but just to hold it in place with the finger while applying the next layer if using a brush.

Remember, if you are using a brush, go along a design so as not to lift the paper with the brush during the stroke and thereby spoil the work.

Once all your designs have been cut and you are ready to attach them, soak the paper in clean water until damp throughout. Remove each one prior to placement and lay it on a dry cloth or towel to remove any excess water. The excess may run down the work and cause problems if you don't. Carefully position the paper and press it gently into place using a natural sponge. Fingers can be used but they sometimes give too much pressure. The sponge is more gentle. Take particular care to press down edges to prevent creep of the slip/glaze/pigment bleeding under the mask. Fine designs should be soaked for less time than bold ones as the paper becomes more fragile the wetter it is and the longer it remains wet.

Dipping, pouring, brushing and spraying can all be used with paper as with any mask that is to be removed prior to firing because any excess slip etc. will be removed with the mask. A spray gun if used with too high pressure or too close to the work can lift the edges of a paper mask. More care should be taken with glaze oxides or enamels when removing masks as particles of glaze may fall from the mask surface and contaminate other areas. Also, if the glaze has dried, dangerous dust can be created which the artist may breath in. With slips, the mask is normally removed as soon as the shine has disappeared from the surface. At that point the slip will no longer run but it is soft enough so that the mask does not cause the slip to flake at the edges of the design. This is also a problem with glaze and occurs when the layer has been left to dry too long or is too thick. The slip remaining on the mask still being damp does not tend to flake off and contaminate other areas. Masks with glaze also should be removed as soon as possible. With thin layers like oxides or enamels the mask can be removed at leisure. A sharp point and tweezers are useful to first lift the edge of the paper until the fingers can grasp it. When removing masks from say the inside of bowls, they should be held on the edge so that any material that falls as the mask is being removed will fall harmlessly away.

Try various types of paper to see what fits your own needs. What works well for one person, may not for another. If using the same shape over and over again on a piece of work e.g. stripes, always cut more than you need as some always become damaged during application. The dry process of cutting is always better completed first and then the wet processes of application and slipping should be done. Preparation ready for all stages makes for more successful and fluid work.

Cardboard re-usable stencils of different shapes and subjects are available in books. These are very useful in schools where they save cutting out sheets and sheets of paper. Once the technique has been demonstrated with these, the more adventurous can make their own.

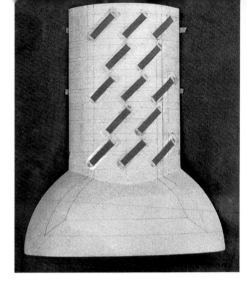

Outline is drawn on the form along with guidelines for stencil placement. This is done in pencil that will burn away. The first stages of stencils are put in place and a gloss black glaze is brushed onto the surface. Painting or airbrush is employed depending on pigments/glazes that are used. Clear plastic book covering film is the mask in this case.

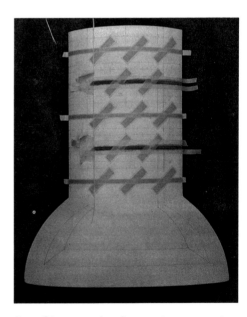

Stencil is removed and protective cover strips applied. Next stage stencil (horizontal stripes) is put in place, glaze brushed on, stencil removed and covered. In this case a flat black glaze is used.

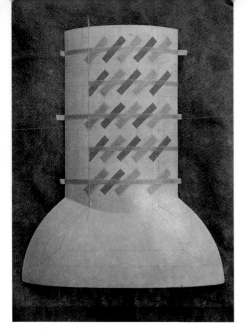

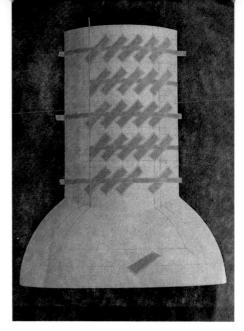

The second series of black glosss rectangle stencils are positioned and painted to complete the grid. The grid is intended to 'hover' in the frontal plane of the finished piece. The black rectangle in the foreground having dropped out of the grid, sits precariously on the illusory edge.

Stencils are removed and covered for protection.

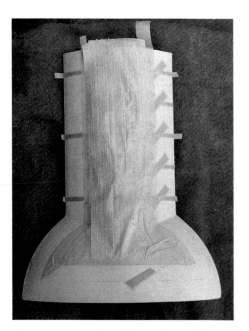

... the application of oil pastel resist. This application is orchestrated to highlight the change of planes within the 'impossible frame' based on central perspective.

The next step involves the masking of the central area, in toilet tissue, to set up for ...

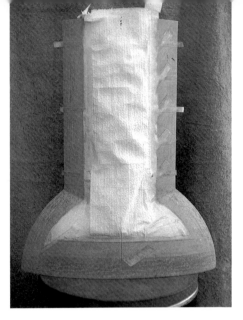

The area is airbrushed with an iron oxide based mixture to pronounce variations within the pastel application. This enhances the warm tones of the pastel and promotes an 'advance' of this area within the total scheme.

Mask removed and side panels of 'frame' are carefully brushed in flat black glaze.

The final stage involves the stripping off all masking and stencils to reveal . . .

The 'impossible frame' is then masked to protect from overspray. An airbrushed application of a brilliant copper blue follows. This visually thrusts the framed black rectangles forward whilst recoiling to the background.

Right
Funnel Vessel (series 2) by Gary Bish (Australia), 36 cm high. Slip cast, 1280°C reduction, using various stencils, wax resist, and airbrush decoration.

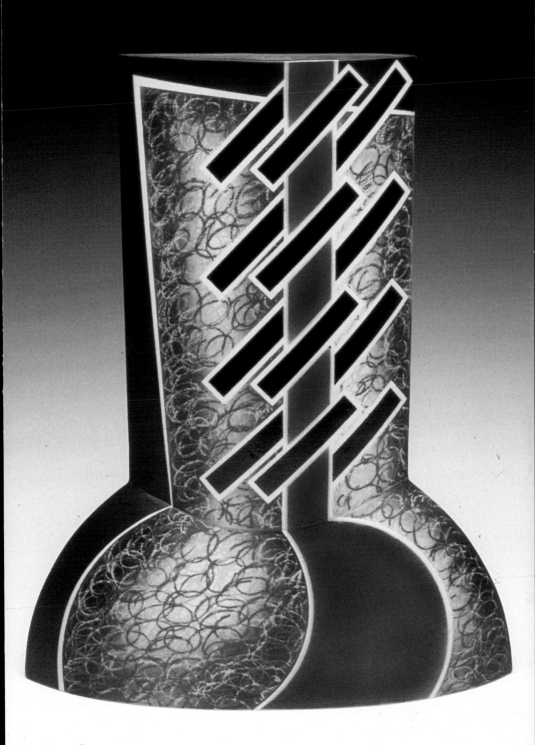

The completed piece ready for firing.

Below
Studio shot with completed piece. (This photographic sequence shows Australian Gary Bish at work.)

Adhesive tapes

Adhesive tapes are generally used on fired glaze or bisque surfaces as they will not stick to a surface which is damp or powdery. As with paper, they were never originally designed for ceramic use so they can be found in a variety of trades and shops. What they all have in common whether they are paper or plastic (the most common) is that they will stick to a ceramic surface and can be removed easily afterwards. If the adhesive is too strong thereby making the mask difficult to remove, try another tape as it is only important that they stick, and easy removal makes for ease of work. If a tape leaves some of its adhesive behind, firing will burn it away, but in some cases the residue can leave an unsightly permanent mark. Solvents such as nail varnish remover or cellulose thinners will easily remove traces. In fine work, use cotton buds. The glue and paper of masking tape can affect colours especially in sawdust firings and can be used to great effect (see section on Jane Perryman on p. 87).

Because the tapes are adhesive, there is less chance of the layer that they are masking creeping under the edge and because they tend to be much stronger than paper, they rarely break when being removed. The plastic tapes mould very easily to curves and can be stretched and moved with ease, unless they are very wide in which case crinkles might appear. These can be removed by slicing them with a knife and them overlapping them. A little gentle heat will make bending and moulding tapes much easier. A hair dryer is a useful tool for this, but it can soften the adhesive too much leaving it behind when the mask is removed.

Every trade from electricians, carpet

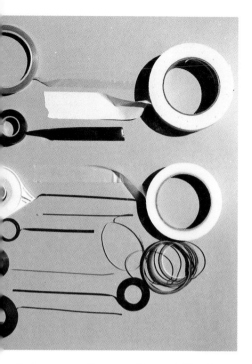

Various types of tape readily available. There are many other types. From top to bottom: Sellotape, masking tape, electrical insulation tape, 'secret tape' (clear tape), tape for putting 'value enhancement strips' on cars, the same, then all split tapes used in the electronics industry.

can give the finest of detail. If tapes need to be cut, they can be stuck down onto glass or shiny plastic sheet for cutting and then peeled off to position on the work without loss of adhesion. Glass is best as it is not marked by the knife whereas plastic is.

Some tapes are more sticky than others and some more stretchy but for a small amount of money a wide range can be purchased with which to experiment. The most versatile and widely used is masking tape bought from any stationers. It comes in a variety of widths from 18 mm to 50 mm but, in general, widths other than 18 mm to 25 mm ($\frac{3}{4}$ inch to 1 inch) have to be ordered unless you go to a specialist graphic supplier. Masking tape can be cut, torn, stretched. It also has a good stick but it is not so powerful that it cannot be used over layers of colour that have already been laid down, but not fired, without damage. However, care is needed. You will read and see later in the book how these can be used.

As a rule masks are removed prior to firing but they need not be. Each person must establish what he wishes to achieve when selecting what process and materials to use.

fitters, painters and decorators, graphic designers to builders has its specifically designed tapes for a particular use. If you keep your eyes open and ask your friends, you will be amazed at the variety of tapes you discover. The graphic design and stationery fields give the widest range of widths and the electronics industry provides the narrowest.

The versatility of tapes lies in the fact that they can be positioned and removed and repositioned so that you can place the mask exactly where you want it. The tapes can be overlapped to build up large areas, they can be cut on the piece to follow the contours in the clay and they

Adhesive papers

Sheet paper with an adhesive back is normally sold in small sheets (A4 or smaller) as label paper. It can then be cut with knives and scissors to the required design and can be drawn on as with paper masks. Adhesive paper is only of real use for large area designs that need to be drawn in one go.

The most useful adhesive paper products are the variety of dots, triangles, stars and other geometric shapes sold in packets for decorating,

Stationery stickers come in many shapes, shown is just a selection, and the masked shapes they leave.

Children's stickers readily available these days and the masked shapes they leave.

identifying, and secretarial situations. They come in a wide range of colours from white to fluorescent but for our purposes it is their stick and shape that is important. Children's stickers in the shape of cartoon characters and animals can also be used (these are usually plastic). Once you start looking, you will find them in all kinds of places.

Adhesive film

These plastic films usually come in a long roll and in different thicknesses depending on their intended use. Film specifically designed for the graphics industry and for use with the airbrush and paints is readily available from good stationers. It can be used in ceramics with the airbrush but with ceramic colours. There are also films made for the signwriting industry for masking out areas for oil-based paints and again these can be used easily for ceramic colours. Suppliers of silk screening products are also a source of films and your local hardware shop too will sell sticky-backed plastic of the types patterned in wood grain to cover old tables etc. These plastic films are all useful when masking.

All films can be cut with a sharp knife or scissors for what ever design is required and they will stick well to glazed or bisque ceramic surfaces. Again, the amount of stick needs to be tested to suit your use. Some films have an adhesive that cures over time (anything from 24 hours) so be sure to complete any work well before a curing time, otherwise the film will be stuck fast and can only be fired away.

Paper and adhesive tapes and films are most suited to smooth surfaces where a clean sharp image is preferred. On textured surfaces it is difficult to get the edges stuck down so there is no creep of the next layers under the edge of the mask. With heavily textured surfaces it would be better to use a resist. All masks and resists can be used with each other and there is the correct one or combination that will suit you. (See Mike Head on page 54.)

Fish Plate by Josie Walter (UK). Paper resist and slip decoration.

b.

Positioning the stencil to insure a good fit before dampening to apply properly.

a. Josie Walter (UK) creating a multi-coloured image with slip using paper resist. a) Cutting out the stencil from drawings done on florists' paper.

c.

Leaves and flowers dampened and in place ready to receive the slip.

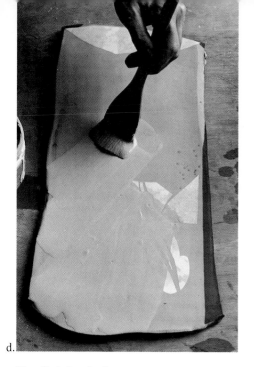

d.

The slip is brushed over.

e.

Other masks to form the vase and the window are placed in position.

f.

The next colour is applied.

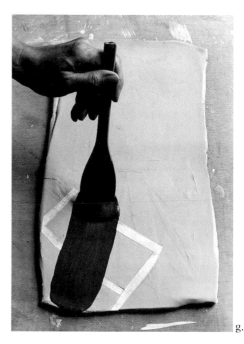

g.

The frame of the window is in place and the black slip applied to form the background. Note how one has to think backwards i.e. the background is put down last.

h.

i.

The masks are lifted with a sharp needle and peeled off, in reverse order of their application.

More masks reveal the design.

j.

k.

Hand decoration is applied, the leaves have been flooded with slip using the ridge left by the mask as a slight wall to contain the slip, saving extra masking.

The finished panel. *All photographs by John Wheeldon.*

Stippling slip through net material.

Removing the net to reveal pattern and texture formed by the slip. *Photographs from Jim Robison (UK/USA).*

Torso by Jim Robison (UK/USA). Constructed piece from panels of clay using various found net stencils and slip to create colour and texture.

Chapter Seven
Exercises in Using Slips and Resists

The use of coloured slips in conjunction with masking techniques is a very good way of building up images and blocks of bold colours. Wax in all forms can be used for very simple work using two colours and latex wax can be utilised to achieve several colours by peeling away the layers of wax for the different applications of colour. However, this has limited use if complex images are required. Using paper or adhesive tapes as stencils gives the greatest variety of possibilities.

There are many different types of masks that can be used and below I describe the techniques to follow to achieve good results. First, the paper must be thin enough that it will lay down well on the surface and not leave gaps at the edge for slip to creep under. This is particularly important on surfaces that are not flat. But having said this, the mask must not be so thin that it will tear when you try to remove it after the slip has been applied – you may ruin the design while trying to pick off the bits of paper. The paper must also be absorbent so that it can be dampened to help it stick slightly onto the surface and therefore not move when slip is applied. Choosing a paper that when damp can be stretched slightly is also most helpful because it will be easier to lay it flat on the surface. The more colours and therefore layers of slip to be used the stronger and thicker the paper needs to be. Playing with different papers soaked

in water and applying them on to curved clay or bisque test tiles will soon show you what potential and suitability they have.

The object to be slipped must be thick enough so that when it absorbs the water from the layers of slip it does not become too wet and distort or disintegrate. Ideally, it should be leather hard so the slip will stick well on the surface. If it is too dry, there is a danger that when the slip dries and shrinks it will flake off and this may not happen until the piece has been fired. To achieve the best fit, the same clay should be used for the slip as for the object so that the shrinkage will be identical. This is not always possible if you are using a dark body and require light or brightly coloured slips. A white slip is the best vehicle for adding colours to give the widest palette.

Vitreous slips can be made up for application onto bisque ware. These are made up in much the same way as any other slip but they should have the addition of a small amount of flux – either feldspar or a frit – which will melt during the firing to 'glue' the slip in place. The amount should be small enough to do the job but still leave the slip with a matt appearance.

The coloration of the slip can be achieved with the addition of clay or glaze stains and oxides in amounts depending on the colour intensity required. Additions of clay or glaze stains should not exceed 20 per cent as this will give rise to problems of the slip not adhering properly to the surface. It will also be found during testing of colours that after the addition of about 15 per cent no real change in colour intensity is apparent and one is just wasting expensive materials.

If the finished object is glazed with a transparent glaze, it may be found that some oxides like copper will bleed into the glaze thereby blurring the crisp image. If this happens, then a clay/glaze stain may be preferred to achieve a crisper result.

When first beginning slip work, test out the chosen slip recipes (before the addition of colour) to establish that their qualities are right for your work. Once the slip is chosen, rather than weigh up lots of little batches to add colour to, mix up a large amount, allow it to dry and then weigh this out in 100 gram batches and add the percentage of colour to these. Two per cent, 4 per cent, 6 per cent, and 8 per cent for dark colours and 4 per cent, 8 per cent, 12 per cent and 15 per cent for pale colours would be good starting places.

Slips can be applied by brushing, pouring, spraying or dipping. The consistency is a matter of choice but if it is too thin, the colour of the slip below may show through and if it is too thick, it may be difficult to remove the paper mask with out tearing the edges of the slip which could leave a ragged line or a ridge around the design showing the thickness. This ridge will be softened when glazed. This ridge can be desirable as the 'valley' left by the paper can be used to drop and flood slip into.

It is best to start by applying paler colours, and working up to the darkest so that there is no danger of dark slips showing underneath pale ones. If the clay body of the object is not white, lay down a layer of white slip first as this will help to make the colours brighter.

Creating the design

I will start off describing a simple image using two colours and then take that further for multi-colour application. In all resist and masking techniques, one must think carefully about the image you require. In many cases, you must think in the negative, e.g. if the background is white and you wish to have black dots, you don't cut out and lay down dots as masks but lay down a sheet with the dots cut from it and then slip with black. You could also lay down the black slip first, then apply dots and cover with white slip and on removing the dots reveal the black below. However, this is not a good way to proceed as has been said, as the black slip may show through the white giving a dirty colour. It is really better to reverse whatever image you want, putting the white down first to give bright colours and the background second.

So let's take a criss cross image as our goal. First sketch onto the paper the drawing in the scale that will fit on the piece, in this case a tile. A white slip will already have been applied over the whole area as a ground and this can be applied thick or thin, textured or with brush marks to add interest to the design. Cut out the rectangles from the drawing and soak them in water ready for application. Pour over the tile the layer of the pale coloured slip and allow it to dry until the shine has gone off and your finger will not leave a mark when lightly pressed on the surface. Now position the dampened but not wet rectangles and press them down with a sponge so that the edges make good contact with the tile and there are no air bubbles. If the sponge overlapping the mask damages the slip already applied and this is not helpful, then use fingers or soft brush.

Now pour the darker slip over the masks and when the shine has gone off, the paper rectangles can be lifted with a needle or sharp knife and fingers leaving the two-colour grid pattern. Care must be taken that the paper is not washed off or moved by the pouring slip. If the slip is left too long and dries too much, the paper will tear the edge of the slip when it is lifted off. If the lines were to be pale and the rectangles dark, then the other part of the drawing would have been laid down after the light slip had been applied. If this had been the case, to form a grid on a curved surface it would have been better to use strips of paper as they would have fitted better onto the surface without creasing. You can also cut darts in the paper to help them fit in a manner similar to that used in dressmaking but remember to overlap the darts.

Now let's take a more complex image of a bunch of pink flowers in a blue and white vase in front of a blue window with a yellow frame on a black background. (See photo sequence on pp. 78–80). First, sort out the colours – lightest first so the colour sequence for application might be: white, pale blue, yellow, pink, green (for the leaves) and black. Draw out your image on the paper and cut out the components.

Dampen each component of the picture when ready for use. The tile should have been previously primed with white slip. As the vase of flowers is in front of the window, it must be in position first. (The colour you wish a shape to be, that is the slip to be put on the tile before that particular mask is positioned.) Brush or pour the blue slip over the tile. When this is touch dry, put the window panes and vase in position. Dip each piece of paper in clean water. Remove excess water with a sponge or towel, position the paper on the tile and smooth it down firmly to remove any air bubbles. Leave it for a few minutes so that the paper will adhere firmly to the clay. Make sure that no parts of the paper have lifted up or the next layer of slip will creep under it and ruin that crisp look. If the paper is too wet, it will slide about when the next layer of slip is applied. Apply the yellow slip and put the window frame in position. Apply the pink slip and put the flowers in position. Then apply the green slip and the leaves, and then cover the whole thing with the black slip. Remove the paper using a needle, sharp knife and tweezers in reverse order (leaves, flowers, frame, panes and vase). Decorate the vase.

Because the colours in slips are expensive, you may not wish and indeed it is not necessary to pour the slips over all the piece but just in areas where it is needed. However, this could leave a ridge so each person must judge whether it is better to put each layer all over. Further decoration of the image by hand can be done if required for small areas that are not worth masking, the flower yellow stamens for example. A black outline could be slip trailed.

The way the colours are ordered has meant that the vase which is at the front of the picture is three layers deep and this may make it look sunk into the picture, so it may be better to do the white ground, the blue window, then black but mask out the vase, flowers and window as one image. This will leave the vase etc. as a white area onto which can be built up its colours by first masking out the black. Experiment yourself.

Points to watch are that the paper must be strong enough to be removed through the layers of slip without tearing, that the slip is not so thick that you cannot see where the paper is (you can use your memory) and that the paper is removed before the slip becomes so stiff that it tears the image when being removed. This can particularly affect thin lines. Of course, it is always possible to touch up mistakes with a brush.

This technique can be used for coloured glazes but there is more likelihood of the edges becoming ragged as the glaze tends to dry too quickly. However, this could be made a feature of the image.

Craig Martell (USA)

The vessels that Craig makes are designed to create an interest in the piece from a distance and to engage the viewer even further as they are seen close up. Craig discovered early on like so many people who use masking techniques, especially with masks that need to be stuck onto the surface, that the smoother the surface the more successful the result. He uses a porcelain clay on his thrown vessels and the masking is all done after they are bisque fired. The pots are turned very carefully to give a smooth surface using metal kidneys with a final burnishing.

He uses a range of tapes and stick-on films, in fact anything that will give him the result he desires. The main tape used is masking tape that comes in a variety of widths from $\frac{1}{16}$ inch (2 mm) to 4 inches (10 cm). He employs a tool bought commercially known as 'The Griffhold Dual Cutter' which holds two blades parallel, so that when run along a tape that has first been stuck to a smooth board, parallel wavy lines can be cut.

Porcelain vase by Craig Martell (USA), 21 inches high. Patterns created using adhesive stationery shapes and strips cut with 'Griffhold Dual Cutter'.

This tool allows lines from $\frac{1}{16}$ to $\frac{5}{8}$ inch (2 mm to 15 mm) across to be cut. The faster the cut is executed, the more fluid the shape achieved. Once he has assembled a vast array of shapes, these can then be selected to fit the form being decorated. Although he has a strong idea of what the design will look like, once the tapes begin to be applied, the form itself will begin to suggest necessary alterations. These are cut directly on the piece, rather than cutting to size before application. Stickers available from stationers, in the form of dots, rings, etc., are also employed.

Some pieces have coloured slips sprayed on while still leatherhard in areas that will be masked out later. These are bisque fired, masked as above and then sprayed with a black glaze. It is important for him to use a glaze that will keep a hard edge during firing to keep the crispness of the design. His pieces that do not have coloured slips put on in this way are sprayed with a dark blue slip, the masks removed and then sprayed with an ash glaze with a bold spray to give an orange peel texture much like salt glaze.

One of the problems he has encountered is that the tape can pull off the coloured slips put on in the clay stage. This can be alleviated by the addition of a small amount of flux into the slip or by soaking the bisque firing for an hour to make it fuse that little bit more. Some tapes do have adhesive that is too powerful and it is a case of searching for a better alternative.

Chris Jenkins (UK)

Chris Jenkins makes thrown pots of simple form using strong linear decoration to complement their quietness and strength. This work

started in the 1970s with experiments to discover how the lines visually twisted, compressed and altered the forms but at the same time complemented them.

Chris uses a mixture of wax and masking techniques depending on the complexity of the pattern. The use of masking has allowed him to have a strident interaction with the form and at the same time enable minute adjustments to be made to the balance of the pattern and form before applying further layers of slip and glaze. He uses newspaper mostly. Sheets are attached to a smooth board with masking tape and then he cuts as many stripes and shapes of the necessary size all in one go (in the case of fine stripes it is important to cut along the grain of the paper or they will easily break). It is better to cut more stripes than are needed so as to have spares. These are then soaked in water and floated onto the leatherhard piece with a flat sable brush. Newspaper is particularly useful in thin strips as it can be brushed accurately into complex curves without crinkling if you use the correct amount of water. The paper resist is pressed down tight with a moist sponge when the design is finished. Failure to do this means the slips can bleed under the edge destroying the clean lines.

The slip is dipped or brushed on top. In the case of brushing he has found it better to paint complex detail with a first coat in the direction of the pattern before banding a heavier layer. This first layer seals the mask tightly in place and directional brush work lessens the chance of the brush dragging the mask from its intended position.

If the pattern consists of large areas, a frame can be formed with paper strips and the central area infilled with wax. This can be used on both leatherhard

clay and bisque ware. Sometimes he covers the whole vessel with adhesive tape and then cuts away areas where slip or glaze is to be. Once the slips have set (the shine has gone from the surface), the paper can be lifted at the corners and peeled away using tweezers or fingers to reveal the surface below. If the slip is left too long, the edges can flake when removing the mask.

When using porcelain and the image is to be mainly white with black lines, the areas to be black are cut from paper, attached to the surface as described above, and then the whole piece is coated in water-based wax. When dry, the paper can be removed revealing the body below. The slip or glaze can then be brushed or dipped taking only where the paper was. The secret of success is to have slips of just the correct consistency. If they are too thick, they will not resist well. If slip or glaze droplets remain on the wax surface, these can be removed with a small damp sponge.

Thrown dish by Chris Jenkins (UK), 14 inch diameter. Mask using strips of newspaper, manganese slip and pale glaze.

Jon Middlemiss (UK)

One of the major areas of interest in Jon's work is the relationship between the hard-edged, dynamic, linear energies of the surface and the subtle gently curved, formal qualities of an object, balancing masculine and feminine. He aims for a particularly crisp linear quality when masking areas of a piece, sometimes in order to accentuate the tension and vitality and at other times to soften, calm, and reintegrate disparate qualities.

Because of this, the techniques he uses must give him reliable visual accuracy, sustainable throughout the subsequent multifiring processes. After the wet piece has been thrown, turned and reassembled, the form is carved and sanded to refine the shape and bring out the texture of the clay. Most of this

Bowl by Jon Middlemiss, 11″(h) × 12″(w).

refining is done when the piece is dry. The pieces are bisque fired before any masking is undertaken. After bisque firing several layers of engobe, thin slip or glaze is painted or sprayed on to create the ground colour and texture. The piece is then refired to harden the surface after which the masking can begin.

To create the curves and lines on Jon's work, it is important that the mask can be cut with a high degree of accuracy and also can be bent to follow the curves without creasing. He has found that self-adhesive vinyls are the most suited to his needs. They are easily cut, retain their shape, however thin the line, and yet can be bent if gently warmed. They are readily available from most decorating/ DIY stores and come in a variety of different colours and textures. Having vinyls of different colours can be useful when creating very complicated patterns to identify what masks go in what area, a bit like painting by numbers. Some have a slight stipple giving a more receptive surface for sprayed glaze, as being nonporous the liquid spray has a tendency to run down the mask onto areas where it is not needed and the stipple tends to hold it. Some brands have a thicker layer of adhesive and so are better for applying to textured surfaces, though they are less useful for delicate work.

Layers of glaze are built up by masking, spraying and refiring, making sure that the hardening on firings are close enough to the final firing temperature to prevent the mask pulling off the previous layer beneath it. After the final layer has been applied, the piece is fired to full temperature (Cone 9, 6 or 4) depending on what glazes have been used.

Jane Perryman (UK)

Jane has been experimenting and perfecting her technique for many years and although quite simple in theory, precise knowledge of her materials and firing enables her to produce her beautiful patterned forms. As with other artists' work it is the effect of smoke and its ability to penetrate though a porous surface to alter the colour of the object below that creates her effects.

The pieces are hand-built using wide flat coils and when stiff enough, scraped to refine the final form. Layers of differing coloured slip are painted over the surface before burnishing and bisque firing to 980°C. The patterns are created using masking tape cut or torn to shape and stuck to the surface. Once they are all in place, a course clay slurry (Potclays crank mix clay) is coated all over the surface to act as a slight barrier to the smoke firing.

The heat and smoke produced during the firing not only penetrate the slip but cause the masking tape to combust. Because it is held in place by the slurry, it carbonises slowly and in so doing affects the surface of the vessel in a different way to the non-masked areas. The glue on the tape enhances this coloration to give subtle hues of colour within a regimented pattern. The tape can lift slightly at the edges during the firing allowing smoke to penetrate under the edges thereby adding to the subtlety of pattern.

The thickness of the slurry has a bearing on smoke penetration as does the speed and fuel used during the firing. Sawdust in different grades and newspaper are used and can be controlled to burn at different rates. All

Vase by Jane Perryman (UK), 43 cm high. Coiled vessel using masking tape mask, smoke fired.

Slurry being painted over the bisque fired and masked piece.

Coiled, burnished and smoked pot by Jane Perryman, 34 cm high.

Scraping away the now fired slurry and burnt masking tape after firing to reveal the subtle colours below.

these combinations will affect the finished effect. The firing takes place in a loosely built brick container.

After firing the slurry that is now bisque fired is carefully scrapped away along with the masking tape that is now blackened, burnt or ash. The piece is then washed carefully, dried and waxed to bring out the depths of colour.

Chance plays its part in such techniques but control and understanding tame this aspect.

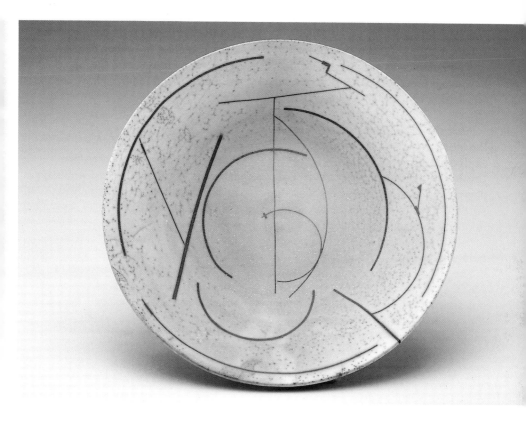

Sara Carone (Brazil)

Sara Carone is another artist who uses
masking in conjunction with sawdust
firings, relying on the ability of smoke to
blacken clay to different intensities
depending on the material it comes in
contact with. Her thrown pieces, once
turned, are burnished using the flat face
of steel kidneys while the piece revolves
on the wheel. They are then allowed to
dry and bisque fired in a reducing
atmosphere to alter the colour of the clay
from its normal overall bland colour to
one of varying hues associated with
reduction firing. This coloration will
remain through the final firing adding
extra interest in the work. A variety of
fine clays of different colours are used.

Drawings are prepared to determine
the designs. These are then transferred

Thrown vessel by Sara Carone (Brazil).
Sawdust fired using various 'split tapes' used
in the electronics industry.

onto the object using oil crayon, litho
pencil, various adhesive tapes of different
widths and split tapes. Split tapes are
very fine, strong, adhesive tapes used in
the electronics industry to lay out
designs of printed circuit boards. They
can be bought from electronic suppliers.

After masking out the design, a layer
of slip is applied followed by a glaze. The
first layer is a mixture of kaolin and
water the thickness of which is varied
depending on the result required. The
second layer, the glaze, is a simple
manufactured alkaline frit. Again the
thickness of this affects the final result.
Thin kaolin and thick frit gives crackles
and dots. Thin kaolin plus thin frit gives

crackles, dots and grey tones. Thick kaolin and thick frit give crackles with dots surrounded by a grey halo. Some kaolin can be added to the frit to give a less fluxing coat which will also alter the effects.

After the application of the two layers, the tapes and masks are removed to expose the clay body and then refired in sawdust. The firing is a very controlled operation with the pieces being placed in particular ways to enable the application of sawdust during the firing to give areas of the kiln higher or lower amounts of reduction.

The firing takes three hours to reach 850°C where the frit will melt and then it is allowed to cool to 520°C. The lid of the top-loading kiln is removed and small bags of sawdust are placed around the pieces. Sometimes the sawdust touches the pots or is just placed near. At other times, a piece is completely smothered depending on the intensity of reduction required. Some pieces are placed on stilts so that the smoke and sawdust can get to their bases while some other pieces have been leant against refractory bricks during the firing. This has the effect of varying the temperature on different parts of each vessel which in turn has the result of causing the frit to be in different states of flux and therefore making it more or less receptive to the effects of the smoke. The more the frit has fluxed, the more resistant to the smoke it is.

The subtleties of colour variation result from the very careful final firing. Decisions about the placement of the work are taken before any decoration has taken place. This also means the pieces need to be handled as little as possible thereby lessening the chance of damaging the delicate coatings. Once the kiln has cooled, the pieces are removed

and the frit/kaolin layer can be peeled away revealing the subtle pigmentation below. The areas where the tapes had been placed and removed have turned jet black.

Patrick Siler (USA)

Patrick Siler interprets everyday experiences through the drawn image. He is neither interested in realism nor a particular style but strives for movement, humour, and the real essence of a situation. To quote, 'You have probably heard of visual shorthand – that magical stuff found in the works of great artists, from the understated masterpieces of Oriental brushwork to expressionist paintings. That is what I want.'

His powerful images are produced with simple stencils and slips and sparing quantities of glaze. He began using blotting paper for his stencils but he found that it was difficult to cut and that it lost too much strength when wet. He now uses butcher's paper on which the image will be drawn many times until correct, before cutting it out with a craft knife. (It will be found that any stencil work can take many hours of cutting if a complex image is required, where as the clay process using the stencils i.e. brushing over slip or glaze can take a matter of minutes.) Patrick cuts out all the stencils needed for a piece before commencing the clay work. This is always good procedure so that the flow of the work can take place uninterrupted.

The objects are made from a heavily grogged clay with lots of 'tooth'. This is

Right
'Jivin man Jim comes to the bar' by Patrick Siler (USA), 98 cm high. Slips and stencils, stoneware.

Patrick Siler (USA) cutting out stencils for a piece of work.

beaten into slabs with his hands and left to cure for two or three days until stiff but still retaining some flex. Then they are cut and assembled into the form. A base slip which is black is brushed over the surface of the leatherhard object and left to dry to the touch. The stencils are immersed in water until saturated. This will make them pliable so that they will stretch enough without tearing to fit the contours of the clay thus preventing the creep of subsequent slip layers under the edges. Excess water is removed from the stencil with a towel or blotting paper before being pressed gently onto the surface.

A second layer of light coloured thick slip is painted over the stencils and black base slip with large brushes which leave traces of the brush movement in the surface. A further layer is added in areas before the previous one has dried so that there is a merging and softness of colour which contrasts with the hard edge of the stencil. These top layers have pigments added to give colour variation as desired. When the slip is dry to the touch, the stencils are removed revealing the black graphic image below. The pieces are dried slowly over weeks, they are then sprayed sparingly with a clear glaze wash and once fired to cone 5–7 in an oxidising atmosphere that is verging towards reduction. Patrick has found that this type of atmosphere gives the best colour response.

Wetting a stencil to soften the paper to make it stick and make good contact with the surface.

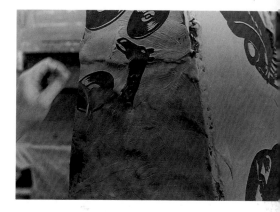

Removing stencils from the piece to reveal the design.

Stencils removed, the finished piece is ready to dry.

Chapter Eight
Colloidal Slips

Colloidal slips are different from normal slips in that they are made of particles which are very much finer than those usually found in normal slips and this in turn gives them a dense quality. Of course, they can be used as normal slips to create many forms of decoration. Indeed, the Greeks used colloidal slips, or terra sigillata as it is sometimes called, to create their famous 'Black Figure ware'. The Romans also used them on their Samian ware. And today, modern artists such as Duncan Ross use them in conjunction with masks and resists. However, the dense nature of colloidal slips means that they can also be used as resists in their own right – though not perhaps in the conventional sense that they are applied to an object, another process takes place and then they are removed. Instead, when the dense colloidal slip is used with clays that are more porous (even if the slip is made from the same clay), the slip will, for instance, resist the effect of smoke. Also, their fineness means that they will vitrify earlier than the main body so that any colour change that can be achieved in the early parts of a firing will be sealed into the slip. In this way, a whole range of rich colours can be obtained with colloidal slips. It is for these reasons that I have included them in this book.

Nature of the slip

When making a colloidal slip, the object of the exercise is to separate the finest particles out of the clay. These are of the range 0.0001 to 0.0000001 cm. These fine particles have the same predominant electrical charge and thus repel one another if dispersed in a liquid. This is why they are difficult to settle out during the making. A clay (particularly very plastic ball clays) may have in its bulk up to 30 per cent of these particles. Any clay can be used to make a colloidal slip.

Extracting the slip

Extracting the slip is easy although at times laborious. The dry clay is placed in a large container such as a dustbin, mixed with water and allowed to slake down. Use about 35 lb (16 kg) of clay to 30 gallons (137 litres) of water. For experimental purposes just reduce the amounts. A water softener such as Calgon and some organic matter such as 'ox-gall' (two teaspoons) bought from the chemist (pharmacy) are added. The Calgon helps to break down the particles and the ox-gall promotes bacteria growth which also aids this process. The mixture is stirred well every couple of days for the first week and then allowed to settle for a further two weeks. It is important that the mixture is not disturbed when settling as this will cause

Earthenware form by Duncan Ross (UK), 19 cm high. Layers of colloidal slips with patterns created with masking tape between the layers.

the unwanted coarser particles to rise up into the liquid.

After the mixture has settled, the top liquid is siphoned off and then put into transparent containers and allowed to settle further for a week or two. It will then be seen that there are three distinct layers in the containers: a thick layer of sediment at the bottom, a thinner layer of sludge in the middle and a dark layer of liquid at the top. This top layer is the colloidal slip and it should be carefully siphoned off into trays and the water allowed to evaporate. When enough water has evaporated to leave a thick slip, it will be found to have a soapy texture and if left to dry further, it will feel like grease rather than clay. Note – it is possible to aid the settlement of the colloidal slip once the slip is removed from the main batch by the addition of a small amount of acid such as vinegar or as is more commonly used calcium chloride. This causes the slip particles to bunch together thereby becoming heavier and so sinking more quickly. This process is called flocculation.

It is sometimes possible to bypass the weeks of settling by first sieving the slop through a fine sieve and then ball milling this finer clay with the addition of a deflocculant for a period up to 48 hours. Sodium metaphosphate is a particularly effective deflocculant for this. This process grinds the particles down and the result is the finished slip. Alternatively, ball mill the finer clay, then let it settle for 20 hours and then siphon off the top layer.

Using the slip

The slip can be sprayed, painted, poured or dipped. However, make sure that the layer is thin because during the making quartz will have been lost from the clay and as the slip will be under compression once it's been fired, it might flake off if it is too thick.

The flat nature of the clay particles means that the slip will always dry with a glossy finish which is at its best on a smooth surface. This can be polished further with a soft cloth prior to firing. The alignment of the particles also means that the slip will fit almost any body. However, because it is so fine, it does not easily allow the passage of water and therefore if a piece is covered all over with slip, it will take a very long time to dry. The slip can be applied to green ware and bisque but it is better to dampen the bisque before application otherwise there may be pinholing which will not heal as say a glaze does when it's fired.

Colouring oxides and stains can be added to the slip but they are best ball milled first so that they are ultra fine. Four hours is usually enough. The slips on their own give a beautiful range of rich colours in browns and greys and are well worth the time and trouble spent experimenting with them.

Susan Halls (UK)

Susan Halls is an artist who uses colloidal slips. Her work deals primarily with animal imagery although she is currently exploring shoes, clothes, cars and organic forms. The majority of her work is finished using primitive firing techniques and low temperature glazes. This includes sawdust/smoke, raku and low-temperature salt firings. The surface quality of the clays and slips she uses at these temperatures with their matt finishes and earthy coloration well emulate the animal qualities she seeks.

Sue has developed specific resist techniques for each type of firing. The most straightforward of these is the use of colloidal slips that have the property of resisting the carbonisation of the base clay during the sawdust/raku firing because of their particle size.

She applies the colloidal slips to her work by brushing, pouring, spraying or dipping but it must be used thinly to avoid flaking after firing. To obtain the animal skin effects, the slip is poured over the piece in a number of thin coats and when dry enough to handle, areas are sponged away to reveal the clay below. The slip comes off very easily so it is important to handle it carefully and with dry hands. The piece is then fired to 950°C and removed while still red hot and placed in sawdust. The areas not covered in the slip will blacken easily and the slipped areas will tend to craze and pick up the smoke in these small cracks thereby accentuating them.

As well as sponging the colloidal slip from various areas, she also uses masking tape, latex resist and damp newspaper to form patterns associated with striped animals – particularly where hard edge definition is needed. Once these resists have been applied, the colloidal slip is either poured over as before or brushed and sprayed on. The resists and masks are removed before firing.

Pieces that are to have less areas of black are fired in a brick chamber. They are lightly covered in sawdust which is then ignited and allowed to smoulder – but not to flame – until all the sawdust is burnt away. This gives a subtle smoke patterning. These pieces use sheets of clay as masks. The sheets are rolled out

'Contemporaneous Animal' by Susan Halls (UK), 12 cm. Handbuilt with stoneware clay, colloidal slips, using clay masks. Sawdust and raku fired.

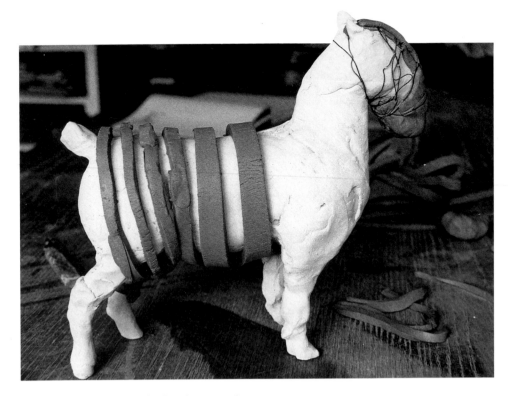

Handbuilt animal, bisque fired with wire and clay masks over colloidal slips, ready for smoking.

Animal in smoking chamber with burning paper.

to about 8 mm ($\frac{3}{10}$ inch) thick which can then be cut into the shapes of stripes or dots to form the animal markings. (It is essential to use grogged clay to lessen the shrinkage and cracking of the soft clay during the firing.) With this technique she works more closely with her detailed drawings as the clay is being used to determine an absence of colour in the areas where it will be applied.

Because the clay masks will not stick to the bisque-fired piece and it will dry to some extent, it is important that the clay can be hooked over some part of the animal or else it will fall off vertical surfaces. There are ways around this problem. For instance, the clay mask could be tied to the clay with a thin wire though you must be careful not to allow the wire to touch the animal's surface or it will leave a line from the smoke and

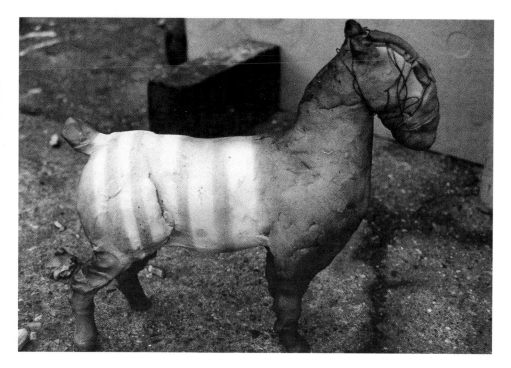

Finished creature with some masks removed. All photographs from Susan Halls.

heat or from the metals in the wire. The piece could also be carefully propped up off the floor of the kiln/smoke chamber so that its weight will not cause the sawdust to push the wire against the animal.

Alternatively, when not using wire, the piece can be laid on its side on a bed of sawdust, which is then set to smoulder, with the clay draped over the now more horizontal surface. Once one side has been done, it can be turned over and the other side patterned. Although the colour of the first side will alter again during the second firing, careful control and experience will keep the sides remarkably similar.

When Sue uses low-temperature salt firings there is a danger that the salt will fuse the clay resist to the object thereby causing damage. In normal salt firings for glazing ware, the pots are separated from the kiln shelves and lids are separated from jars using salt 'wadding' which is a mixture of alumina hydrate (which is not affected by salt) and a small percentage (5–15 per cent) of either china clay or bentonite to make it plastic. This wadding can be moulded like dough, rolled out and cut into shapes to be used as resists. For Sue Halls, the normal recipes are not plastic enough so she mixes the alumina with baking flour to make the dough. The result is not only good to work with but also durable enough to withstand the volatile chemistry of the salt kiln. As with clay resists, it will not hold well on vertical surfaces and it must therefore be draped or hooked over the object to keep it in position.

Chapter Nine
Acid Etching

The use of acid etching was briefly mentioned in the history chapter. The primary reason for using acids is to matt down a glaze surface to give a consistent colour to a piece but with subtle texture changes or to etch through one layer into another of perhaps a different colour. Thin coatings that may hide colours below like all-over lustres can be removed in areas to reveal varying colours below. Greg Daly (Australia) produces work rich in colour which is partly created with the use of acid etching with lustre and gold leaf. The addition of gold leaf to ceramic as in Greg Daly's work sticks better to an acid etched surface than to a shiny one.

The acids that are used are hydrofluoric or bifluoric acid which are acids that eat glass. Bifluoric is sometimes known as 'cream glass'. IT MUST BE STRESSED THAT THESE ACIDS ARE EXTREMELY DANGEROUS – HYDROFLUORIC IS THE MOST DANGEROUS AND BIFLUORIC ONLY MARGINALLY SAFER. BEFORE UNDERTAKING ANY ACID WORK THE USER MUST CONSULT HEALTH AND SAFETY DATA FROM THE SUPPLIER AND FOLLOW IT STRICTLY. THIS INCLUDES THE DISPOSAL OF UNWANTED ACID.

The areas not to be etched need to be masked with a material that will not be affected by the acid – latex, wax, rubber solutions and tapes can be used. Sellotape (Scotch tape) is also resistant to these acids. Lead foil and animal fats are used mostly in the glass industry. Testing should be done first to ascertain the suitability of the resist to be used and the acid manufacturers should be able to supply and recommend appropriate materials. It must be remembered that if you are etching a glazed surface, you must be able to remove the mask easily when the job is done. It is no use using say a rubber solution that you then cannot remove without ruining your work. Although, in some cases, if difficulty does occur and the glaze does not have too low a melting point, the piece can be refired to 600°C to burn the mask away.

Masking can take place in the usual way but you must make sure that if tapes are used, they are close to the surface to prevent creep at the edges. Hydrofluoric acid comes, and is used, in liquid form, usually at 60 per cent strength. Bifluoride is a paste and is not as strong as hydrofluoric; the paste will lessen the danger of creep but it tends to take longer to etch.

Wearing rubber gloves, the acid is painted onto the surface with a brush and left for the desired time. This is dependent on the hardness of the glaze and the strength of the acid. It can be washed off and, if hot wax has been used, this can be dissolved with hot water. A liquid soap is then used to to wash the surface as scumming may occur. If you are at all worried that

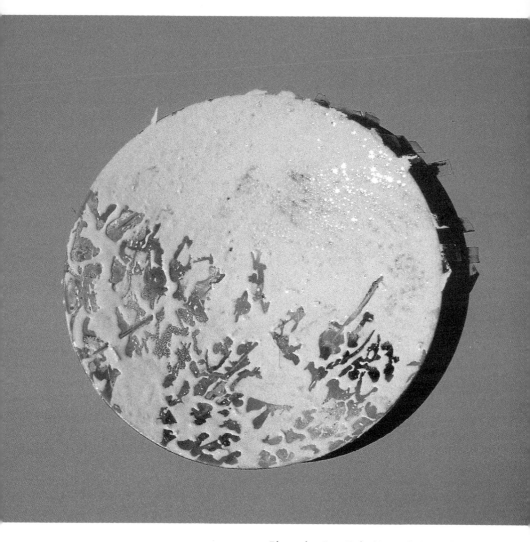

active acid may still be on the piece, then use a neutralising solution as recommended by the acid supplier.

It may be necessary to apply several coats of acid to give the required effect and only trial and error will show this.

Acid etching is only suitable for glazed surfaces and the smoother the glaze the better the results, the results being a frosty but smooth contrast unlike grit blasting where the surface is much rougher. Very textured glazes which will tend to be more matted are not

Platter by Greg Daly (Australia). Masked with 'Sellotape', a clear adhesive plastic tape, and coated with 'cream glass' bifluoric acid paste.

recommended as the results will be too subtle and the acid may be trapped in bubbles or fissures in the glaze and cause injury. If textured glazes are required to be worked on then Grit Blasting (see Chapter Twelve) can be a much better solution.

REMEMBER – BE CAREFUL!!!

Lustre bowl by Greg Daly (Australia). Acid
etched lustre with gold and silver leaf.

Chapter Ten
Lustre Techniques

Lustres have long been used in ceramics to produce a beautiful metallic sheen on glazed surfaces in a variety of colours and most of us buy them from our ceramic supplier mixed in resin ready for use. These metals – usually gold, silver, platinum, copper, bismuth and tin – are dissolved in hydrochloric acid to produce a chloride which is added to sodium resinate to form a precipitate which is then added to an oil medium for ease of application. When a fired glaze is coated with the lustre and refired at a low temperature, the resin content causes the metal to reduce leaving a very thin layer of the pure shiny metal.

Lustres are usually applied to shiny

Bowl by Sutton Taylor (UK). Various lustre techniques.

glazes for best results and the glaze must be able to soften slightly at about 750°C, which is the normal temperature area for lustres, to enable the lustre to stick to or penetrate the glaze.

Normal masking techniques using adhesive tapes and waxing to resist areas can all be used in very much the same way as with other ceramic materials as described elsewhere in the book. Sometimes the medium that a lustre is in can dissolve waxes making them difficult to use and if this is found to be the case, then latex wax should be used. Latex wax is a good material to use with lustres as it is painted easily onto a fired glaze surface, does not run and it peels away readily. All masks should be removed prior to firing lustres in case any ash residue contaminates the softening glaze surface.

Patterns can be painted onto the fired glaze surface with watercolour paint or gouache (straight from the tube and not diluted), allowed to dry and then over-painted with commercial lustre. The clay content of the paints resists the lustre during firing. After firing, the watercolour washes away leaving the lustre pattern in the areas where there was no paint. Paints do contain ceramic pigments but because the firing is so low they are unable to affect the glaze colour. (See Chapter One.)

There are a small band of potters around the world who use lustres in very interesting ways and most of them make up their own lustres for their own particular working methods. These give a more interesting range of colours than can be bought commercially. It must be said that to achieve a result with your own lustres is relatively easy but to have a good range of colours and to achieve consistently good results requires a great deal of testing and a very accurate kiln.

Small temperature fluctuations can easily ruin an effect. The techniques to achieve your own quality lustres are not in the remit of this book.

Masking techniques

Sutton Taylor is an English potter who has achieved superb qualities of work in the lustre field and has given me much of the information for this section. The varied colours and shapes that appear on the surfaces of his work give continued pleasure while being intriguing as to their execution. Below are discussed some of the masking techniques that are peculiar to lustre work.

In-glaze lustres are formed when a suitable glaze containing metal salts is refired to its melting point and held under reduction until the metals convert to their metallic state or colour. For example, a glaze containing copper, green in oxidation, will become red in reduction. By masking parts of the glaze from the reduction gases, red and green patterning can be made. A simple paste of clay, water and gum painted onto the surface makes an effective barrier. If the mask is slightly permeable then a mottled effect can be achieved. Adding coarse sand or grog to the clay paste will allow some penetration of the reduction gases. Deliberate spotting can be achieved by adding combustible material to the clay paste that will burn away during the firing leaving holes that allow the reduction gases to touch the glazed surface. Coffee grounds, lentils, porridge oats, grass, and poppy seeds can all be used. There is no end to the possibilities.

You may ask why the clay paste does not stick to the glaze surface as it melts. The answer is that it often does and it is the greatest hazard with this method. The skill is to fire the glaze to the point where it is sufficiently soft so that the reducing atmosphere can penetrate the glazed surface but not so much as it will hold the clay. A few degrees too high and all is lost as the clay will be irretrievably stuck. Each glaze has its own optimum temperature and it is a matter of experimentation and a very stable, controllable kiln.

Onglaze pigment lustres again use a clay paste but in this case the metal salts are mixed in the clay which is painted onto the surface of an already fired glaze. The piece is then refired to the softening point of the glaze, in reduction, and the metal salts are transferred onto the glaze surface. The salts become chemically combined with the glaze and the reduction retains them in their pure metal form. Again the temperature must be sufficient to soften the glaze but still allow the clay to be removed.

Pigment pastes of this type are difficult to apply and the use of latex and wax resists on areas to be kept clean and free of pigment are a great help to keep the paste in the correct areas while it dries.

Additions can be made to the clay paste as with in-glaze lustres to give mottled effects. Broken textures can be achieved by painting the pigment on top of wax emulsion which is not able to throw off the paste as it would with a more liquid coating. It forms into irregular patches which will be directly reproduced in the firing. All types of tapes can be used to form patterns but they must be removed before the paste stiffens too much or it will flake as the tape is peeled away or at least crumble at the edges.

Vapour lustres are formed by allowing metals to volatilise in the kiln. These then circulate in the kiln gases forming an iridescence on the surface of any receptive glaze they touch. Again any barrier that can prevent the vapour reaching the glaze will prevent this. A clay paste can be used but it is also possible to use household paint or typist's correction fluid which work very successfully because of their clay content.

I have listed general recipes in the back of the book as a starting point for anyone interested. It is misleading to give specific, individual recipes because so many variables are involved which effect the results, from particle size to humidity on the day of firing. Nobody should become involved who is not prepared to experiment widely but the results are worth the effort!

Chapter Eleven
Masking Resists and Smoke

Masking and resist techniques can be used with a variety of firing styles and sawdust and raku firing are particularly suitable for these techniques.

Raw clay masks

One method which is almost exclusive to these types of firing is the use of raw clay masks in various ways to prevent the smoke (whilst reducing the piece) from reaching the surface of the object. Artists such as Jerry Caplan (USA), Dave Roberts (UK) and Kate and Willie Jacobson (USA) have used this technique to great effect.

The process usually involves making a piece with a very smooth or burnished surface that is bisque-fired, and then covering this with a layer of soft clay in the form of a slip. As the clay layer dries it will crack with a series of fine lines and consequently, when placed red hot in sawdust, the smoke will be able to penetrate through the cracks and leave its mark on the vessel as a series of interesting fine black lines.

The main problem is that once the clay layer has dried, it is very fragile and more often than not will fall away either during the firing, while being handled or in the sawdust so that the exposed object will finally emerge as black all over. To overcome this, the layer of clay slip must be applied reasonably thinly and then sprayed or poured over with a layer of low-temperature glaze. The purpose of the glaze is so that when it fluxes it will turn the clay into a crust similar to the shell of an egg. This will be much more resilient when being removed from the kiln and placed in the sawdust for reducing. It will hold the slip in place and it will also be more resilient to smoke penetration when fluxed.

If the formula for the slip is such that during the firing it reaches only a low bisque maturity, when the piece has cooled and is removed from the sawdust, the outer layer should come away easily like peeling a hard boiled egg; any slip that does remain should come off with a gentle scrubbing in water. The resulting pattern of ghostly black crackle lines on a smooth pale surface gives a most beautiful quality. The thicker the slip that is applied, the bigger and less frequent are the cracks i.e. the bolder the pattern. The thinner the slip, the smaller the cracks and the less obvious the pattern.

It should also be noted that the thinner the slip and glaze, the more opportunity the smoke has to penetrate through the layer itself, giving a less-defined but more atmospheric effect on a darker clay ground. By experimenting with different thicknesses on different parts of a piece, you can cause subtle changes in pattern definition to flow around the piece, or perhaps to create small crackles on necks and rims and bolder ones elsewhere. The slip will shrink to some extent but if this is too severe, the problems of flaking at the wrong time will be encountered. Jerry Caplan doesn't use a glaze when using this technique. However, he prevents his very thick slip from falling away by mostly using it on horizontal surfaces.

The glaze used does not have to cover the whole of the surface; the smoke will penetrate successfully through the areas with slip only if the slip is not too thick. Areas can also be masked either before the slip is applied so that the object's surface is always revealed during the process or on the slip to mask the glaze layer to give changes in cracking and smoke penetration.

Tapes and waxes can be used for masking as long as they are able to stick to the surface. Tapes would work well on the burnished bisque surface but less well on the slip layer and not at all on the unfired glaze, where waxes would be the better choice. Damp paper will also work but for any mask if you need to remove it before firing, care and timing is needed to prevent flaking of the edges.

Most of the artists that I have talked to recommend that the glaze should cover large rather than small areas as there is a tendency with small slip and slip/glazed areas to lift and fall away during firing. Choosing the correct slip and very careful handling will alleviate this problem.

Encouraging cracks

It is possible to encourage cracks to develop in a controlled way by marking the surface of the slip before it dries and working it as follows. First dampen the piece so that the slip layer will firm up but still remain soft. Then, using a fine point such as a pin or a pencil or even the likes of stiff hair from a brush, draw the pattern that you want to appear. It is very important that the marks that you make cause a depression to form in the clay, working on the principle that when the slip dries and shrinks and cracks, the cracks will form along the lines of least resistance i.e. where you have made the slip thinner wth your pointed marker.

Care must be taken that you don't cut through the slip layer. If you do, it is likely that when the slip dries, it will flake away in panels the shape of your pattern or that the glaze that is applied to form the crust will be touching the surface of the vessel and will melt onto the surface during firing giving a roughness to areas. Jerry Caplan draws through his slip layer but being on a horizontal surface and handled carefully, it will only fall away when needed.

Once the pieces are finished, they must be dried fully before committing them to the kiln so that any escaping moisture does not blow off the masking layer. Handling the pieces during the firing should be done as little as possible and with great care so as not to dislodge the crusty layer. Using the kiln as the reduction chamber so that the piece is not handled at all with tongs is a good idea. However, only a few pieces could be fired in a day with this method. The use of a top hat kiln could give you better access for handling the hot piece of work. Jerry Caplan has developed a very interesting firing technique to get around this problem. It is described in the section featuring him (see page 113).

Alternatively, the slip layer could be left undisturbed with the drawing of patterns taking place on the unfired glaze layer so that when it fluxes, the smoke will penetrate the slip layer more easily. (See the work of Dave Roberts described on pages 108–10.)

Colour changes

Some masks and resists, if left on the work during sawdust firings, will help to alter the colour quality of the surface. The material of the mask (being either paper, plastic or rubber based) or the nature of the adhesive can all contribute to this effect. This is either caused by localised differing levels of reduction (generated by the variable amount of combustion of the mask) or by the chemical reactions that are caused by the constituents of the masking materials.

Slip layers put over a masked surface to act as a means of holding vapours close to the object's surface can give very exciting results. Masking tape is the most common material used. Jane Perryman produces extremely interesting work in this way. (See the section on Jane Perryman on pages 87–8.)

Dave Roberts (UK)

Dave Roberts has become well-known for his expertly-made raku vessels with their smooth, pale surfaces patterned with dark smoked, linear patterns. Dave Roberts's coiling in itself shows an uncanny level of skill as the vessels appear to have been carefully thrown and turned. Instead, they are coiled using extrusions of white St Thomas clay from Potclays UK with the additon of 6.5 per cent of 20s to dust dry grog. When the smooth pieces are leatherhard, they are coated with a fine layer of levigated slip made from ESVA ball clay (see recipes on page 125) to which stains have been added. The surface is then burnished with a variety of metal and wooden tools and after drying slowly, the pieces are bisque fired to Orton cone 06.

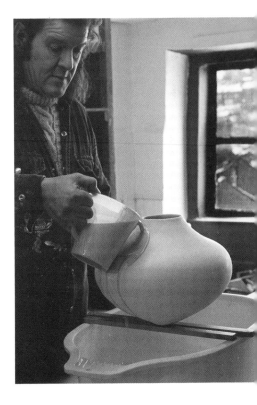

Dave Roberts pouring layers of slip onto the burnished and bisque fired piece.

The pieces are then sprayed with a thick layer of a resist slip to a thickness of up to 3 mm ($\frac{1}{8}$ inch). The slip is made of 3 parts of china clay to 2 parts of flint (by volume) plus 10 per cent copper oxide. The thickness is judged with a pin. Once the piece is thoroughly dried, it is sprayed with a raku glaze (see recipes on page 125). It is important if the process is to work that the glaze layer goes on as a powdery layer rather than a flooded layer and for this reason the work is sprayed from a distance to give the airborne glaze particles a chance to dry before resting on the vessel. The glaze is sprayed on in several layers.

Again, the piece is left to dry thoroughly and then, using pointed tools (he finds a wooden cocktail stick the

Scratching through the layers to create a 'weakness' for the smoke to travel down.

Below
The vessel being removed from the kiln, the slip/glaze layer already beginning to flake away.

Removing the crust to reveal the decoration below. *Photographs from David Roberts.*

Coil-built vessel by David Roberts (UK), 40 cm diameter. Burnished raku using clay and slip mask coating.

most successful), patterns are drawn through the glaze layer to the slip below. If the pot is still damp or if the glaze layer was flooded on when the patterns were drawn, the glaze will tend to flake off leaving a ragged edge which will spoil the finished result. When done correctly, the pattern initially can look quite crude but once fired becomes wonderfully sensitive.

The pieces are fired one at a time to 850–910°C, then removed from the kiln while still red hot, placed in a container (such as a metal dustbin) which can be sealed and smothered in sawdust or straw to achieve a good reduction.

During the firing, the outer glaze layer will have melted and the resist slip bisque fired. The slip will also have shrunk slightly and, as it no longer fits over the pot, begun to crack. Because the melted glaze is holding it together, the cracks will appear where the pattern was drawn through the glaze i.e. at the points of least resistance. In the reduction chamber, the smoke is able to travel down these cracks, causing black lines to be formed on the surface exactly echoing the original lines drawn. When the piece is cool, the resist slip layer will peel away like an egg shell revealing the smoked pattern. After washing, the pieces are waxed and polished to reveal and enhance all the subtle colours produced by the smoke, stains and copper in the slip.

Kate and Willie Jacobson (USA)

Kate and Willie Jacobson are another team of artists who utilise the ability of smoke during a raku firing to penetrate through a layer of slip and glaze to pattern the surface of their work. Their pieces are first thrown, turned and burnished. Then they are bisque fired to 900°C in the normal way. A layer of slip is applied by brush over the surface, allowed to dry and then a glaze of milky consistency is poured over it. The pieces are then ready for the final firing.

If strong, definite patterning is required, then masking tape cut to shape is applied to the piece before the slip and glaze are applied. They have also used wax twine wound around pieces and

'Spirals' by Kate and Willie Jacobson, 22 inches high. Tapes and latex removed before raku firing. *Photograph by Peter L. Bloomer.*

Windsor and Newton watercolour masking fluid (which is a latex rubber-based liquid) to great effect. The masks are removed as soon as the glaze has been applied and while it is still damp enough to prevent flaking at the edges of the pattern when the tape is pulled away. This leaves a good crisp image.

The firing to 700°C melts the glaze at which stage the piece is removed and placed in a smoking chamber with sawdust to produce the smoke required to blacken the areas which have been masked out but are now exposed. The slip which is now bisque fired has shrunk on the surface of the piece and cracked but is held in place by the melted glaze. The smoke can therefore penetrate these cracks to the piece below giving the characteristic black crackle lines. The piece, once cooled, has the glaze and slip peeled away to reveal the pattern.

In some of the Jacobsons's pieces, the slip is coated all over but the glaze is then applied with a slip trailer in broad, bold movements to form spiral glazed areas. After firing, the result is pale crackle curves where the glaze had been and black curves where there was only slip as the added glaze layer is more resistant to the smoke.

The Jacobsons's method is similar to the method used by other artists but with the use of different masking and resisting materials, variations in technique and an individual approach to form, a wide range of styles and possibilities are available from different experts.

'Necee Regis' by Jerry Caplan (USA), 21 inch diameter. Reduction stencilling raku drawing.

Jerry Caplan (USA)

Jerry Caplan has developed a variation of the standard raku technique that employs the use of clay stencils on bisque ware, particularly bowls and plates. The pieces are reduced with the minimum of smoke in a reduction chamber using a technique he calls 'smokeless raku'.

Since clay shrinks as it dries and since wet clay will not stick to bisque ware, he is able to pour slip into a bowl, rinse it around to coat the inside and pour off the excess, leaving a layer that is the clay stencil. The slip used for the stencil is usually the same as the body of the bowl but it is blunged to give it a creamy consistency and sieved through a 60s mesh sieve to remove all the grog. He is able to draw the required design through this stencil.

The bowl which has been fired to Cone 08 has considerable porosity and sucks the clay stencil to itself. As it firms up, it loses its gloss and takes on a leathery quality. It is at this point, using a potter's needle, that the drawing can be inscribed into the clay coating to the bowl below. As the stencil continues to stiffen, he is able to remove whole areas cleanly thereby creating strong patterns of shapes acccompanied by line drawings.

The bowl and stencil are allowed to dry for a few days to permit the water that penetrated the bisque to evaporate. He sometimes force dries them in a domestic oven to hurry along the process. When dry, the stencils are very fragile and the bowl must be treated with care to avoid shifting the pattern.

The dry piece is then placed in an ordinary kiln and fired to 650°C. Once it has reached temperature, the kiln is switched off and the piece removed using raku gloves (not tongs as the gloves give more control and thereby lessen the risk of disturbing the stencil). Meanwhile, the reduction site has been prepared on a flat piece of ground which has a piece of kiln shelf on it to protect it from the hot bowl. The reduction chamber is an ordinary strong cardboard box that is larger than the piece to be reduced. A ring of sand is placed on the ground into which the rim of the box will be bedded once the bowl is in place. The sand makes a very good seal so that little combustible material is required and no smoke escapes. The smoke is generated using a sheet of newspaper placed on the floor onto

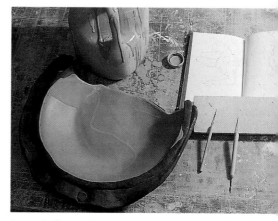

Jerry Caplan with a thick slip coating ready for drawing.

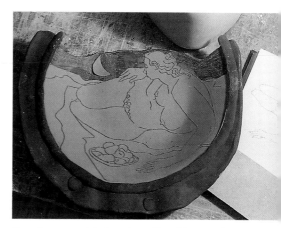

Drawing completed ready to fire. *Photographs by Jerry Caplan.*

'Dancing Figures' by Jerry Caplan (USA), 16 inches across. 'Smokeless raku'.

which the bowl is stood and a second sheet placed on top. The paper ignites immediately so the cover must be quickly placed on top and the box sealed. If smoke begins to seep out, it can be blocked with more sand.

After about 5 to 10 minutes, the container can be removed revealing the burnt paper and the reduced bowl. The bowl can be picked up and the stencil tipped out. It should fall away easily. If it does not, then it can be eased away with

a potter's needle to reveal the black and white design.

Jerry Caplan has made black and white patterns successfully for many years and has now introduced colour into the work by painting Reward Velvetones onto the green ware prior to bisque.

Once the stencil is applied as described, one cannot remember precisely where the colour is so a more spontaneous approach is used. If it is important that the colour and lines match, Jerry first traces the shape of the colour, then applies the slip as usual and by placing the tracing on the clay and drawing over it the surface is embossed with the pattern. It is then a simple matter to use the needle to cut the design as usual.

Most of Jerry's work is on flat pieces because of the danger of the stencil becoming dislodged when handling and firing. He has done some experiments with vertical pieces and has found that the more textured they are the better, as this gives the clay slip something to grip on to. It does however mean that the mask is more difficult to remove after firing and has to be picked at. He is still working to improve the method.

Many variations of this technique can be experimented with using different thicknesses of slip, clay and colours.

Ruth E. Allan (USA)

Ruth Allan makes saggar-fired thrown vessels that are etched and resisted in a variety of ways prior to firing to enhance the pinks and greys associated with this process. The vessels are thrown in procelain clay and when leatherhard are burnished in the usual way to give a smooth surface that is more receptive and sympathetic to the subtle colours that are the hallmark of saggar firing. The pieces are then treated in a variety of ways depending on the result required.

At the green ware stage areas are

Burnished vessels by Ruth E. Allan (USA). Burnished, tape and wire masks. Saggar fired.

painted with a good quality wax resist or shellac onto bone dry pots. When the wax or shellac is dry, using a rather wet natural sponge, the surface of the piece is wiped repeatedly. This removes the clay from the areas not coated. As the piece begins to get too wet, it is allowed to dry before further sponging. Latex wax because of its rubbery nature does not work well with this technique as it tends to peel away.

This etching technique can be used to create significant depths in the clay surface; the sponged areas can be reburnished with a dry cellulose sponge to bring the surface back to match the rest of the vessel. Stains and coloured slips can be added to the surface before wax is applied over them or after the sponging has been finished. For example, if an area is waxed, then sponged, then black slip applied, once the piece is fired the result will be a black and white design with the raised areas being white. If the black slip is under the wax, the reverse is the result. When sponging dry clay, care must be taken that the piece does not crack as the introduced water expands the clay. This is particularly prone to happen on thin rims. Trial and error is the only solution.

The now dry pieces are bisque fired in the normal way. She then wraps very fine copper wire around them and applies pieces of torn masking tape onto areas of the surface, utilising these to hold the wire in place. The pieces are than placed in a saggar built up of fire bricks inside a gas kiln. The pots are surrounded by sawdust, wood shavings and salt placed in areas to react with the pots during the firing to Cone 012–04. The range of firing alters the quality of the colour and the temperature is chosen depending on the pieces being fired. Great care must be taken when packing the saggar so that the correct amount of salt works on the pieces. Too much salt can cause cracking as can too rapid a firing. It has taken Ruth many years to perfect her technique to give the required effects with a minimum of cracking.

During the firing the shavings burn, and the salt vaporises and colours the surface with cloud-like effects. The attached wire gives off its copper content leaving strong linear marks with a haloed edge and the masking tape, as it slowly burns, seems to attract minerals that are floating around in the saggar with the salt to give patches of added colour. Different tapes will give different results as the composition of the tape varies. Steel wool and ceramic fibre are also utilised as 'soft' masks between the pieces when packed in the saggar.

Saggar firing is a very difficult technique to control and extensive testing is needed to achieve good consistent results.

Chapter Twelve
Grit Blasting

Grit blasting is in a sense another form of spraying but instead of colours and glazes from delicate tools like the airbrush, a jet of abrasive sand or grit is forced onto the object's surface at high speed. The sand used most extensively used to be silica sand in a variety of particle sizes but this is now banned in industry for health reasons. (I assume because of the dangers of silica dust to the lungs.) Aluminium oxide, aluminium silicate, iron silicate and oliviene sand are now commonly used. The blasting materials are extremely hard and when the particles hit the ceramic, or other hard material, each particle bites away a small piece of the suface leaving a little crater. If the gun is held in one spot for any length of time it will very soon, depending on the hardness of the surface, wear a hole through the piece.

Having said this, various sizes of gun and fineness of sand are available and remarkably fine work can be achieved, particularly with the use of suitable masks.

Depending on the result required, grit blasting can be done on clay in all stages from wet through to fired glaze.

Clay surfaces

With wet clay being soft, and with leatherhard, there is a tendency for the sand to be imbedded in the clay as it eats away at the surface and the results tend to be rather hit and miss in quality and effectiveness.

Effects of grit blasting on a clay tablet. The grit will very soon erode a hole through the thick dry clay.

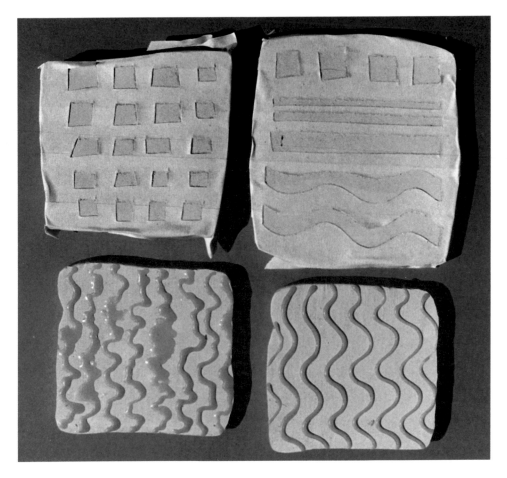

Masking tape and latex as masks on unfired clay.

Damp eroded particles will tend to prevent the dry grit from flowing easily from the gun and blockages may occur. In general, the drier the material being abraded the better; the grit should always be used dry. Using the gun on soft clay without masks tends to ruffle up the surface rather like the sand patterns found when the tide goes out. The same effects can be achieved using just compressed air, so the addition of grit would only be a consideration if the grit added an effect in either texture or fired colour.

On dry clay, the grit will eat its way through the surface VERY quickly particularly in thin walled sections. The force of the stream can quite easily break edges or crack thin walled objects but experimentation will determine how thin one can go.

This technique gives a very distinctive texture to the surface of clay and the coarser the clay or the grit being fired, the more textured the surface. Freehand patterning can be achieved but more successful results are obtained with masks. The effects are not easy to obtain by other methods.

Bisque ware can be treated in much the same way as with dry clay and being

The tablets grit blasted. Because the masking tape does not stick well to dry clay, the air pressure has lifted it from the surface. The latex is now matt.

harder, there is more time for consideration of the effect the grit is having. Also, as the pieces are stronger, they are less likely to be broken while handling. They can be high fired after treatment with or without a glaze. They usually are more effective without any glaze as any subtleties in texture will not be lost under the glaze surface.

Translucent porcelain may be an interesting candidate for exploration during the bisque stage to give subtle changes in thickness and light absorption when high fired in much the same way as Jeroen Bechtold achieved with shellac and sponging on page 22.

Work that has been built up with different all over layers of coloured slip can then be eroded to reveal the different colours and layers below. With coarser grits these layers will be more interestingly textured.

On glazed ware there is the scope to matten a glaze to give all over colour but with different finishes. You can also put on different layers of coloured glazes and eat through one layer to another. Or,

you could go completely through the glaze layers to the clay below and further on through the clay as well. If the body is an interesting colour, this can look very arresting.

Note: The clay body of glazed ware must not be vitrified if it is to be eaten into because if the clay has become harder than the grit the surface will remain unscathed.

Blasting gun

The blasting gun is a specialist piece of equipment with a very hard tungsten carbide nozzle to protect it from the abrasiveness of the sand and different sized nozzles can be purchased for different grit sizes and delicateness of requirements. Never ever try to use your glaze spray gun as an experiment – it will be ruined in seconds. Coarse grade

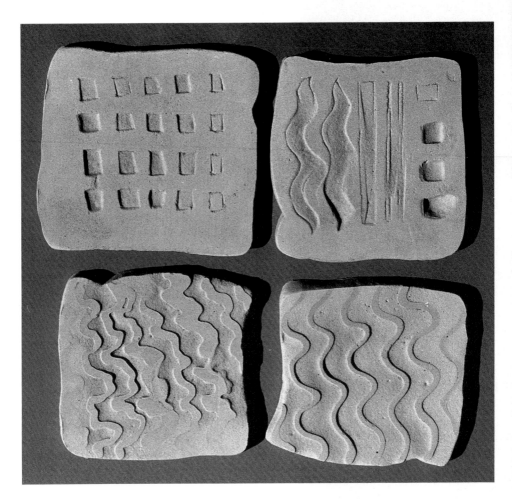

The masks removed, the latex image is crisp but the tape has allowed the grit to creep under giving a fuzzy image.

equipment can be hired as it is used in building renovation for cleaning stone and brick work. Manufacturers will give demonstrations of their equipment. If you already have a good compressor for your glazes, then you are half way there. It must be able to give a pressure of at least 40 psi; airbrush compressors are not powerful enough.

As can be imagined the sand coming out at such high pressure gets everywhere and it is usual for the work

to be done in a sealed cabinet so that the sand can be recycled. This is important as it comes from the gun in great volumes and it is too expensive to waste in such quantities. The sand in the cabinet is sucked back into the sand reservoir through a grill in the base. The cabinet has a toughened clear window and heavy, sealed-in rubber gloves entered with the hands from outside to hold the work and also to protect the skin from severe abrasion. The sand swirling in the cabinet does obscure viewing to some extent.

Most art colleges have blasting cabinets with which you can

Masking tape and latex as masks on bisque clay tablets.

The tablets grit blasted, the masking tape sticks better to this surface so does not lift.
However, being harder the edges of the tape begin to erode.

Masks removed, the image is crisp but not so deep being a harder material than unfired clay.

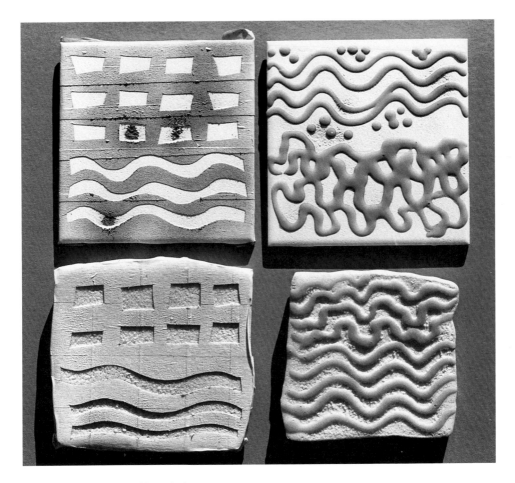

Glazed tiles masked and blasted, the top is hard glaze, the bottom is soft thick glaze. In some areas, the glaze has been completely eroded away.

experiment, given permission, before buying your own. The equipment is expensive and it would be possible for the more practical of you to make one from metal or even wood sheet material. Wood is easier to work with but it may not last very long with the abrasive grit. It should be bigger rather than smaller so that the sand has lost much of its velocity by the time it hits the sides. Windows and the correct heavy duty gloves can be purchased from blasting cabinet manufacturers. Basically you

need a box on legs with a window, the gloves, and a door that seals well through which to insert the work. I would not be able to give plans for such a homemade device here and anyone taking on such a project must do their own research.

Large pieces of work can be done outdoors. Care should be taken to wear face and eye protection and to do the blasting in an area where the flying sand is not a problem.

The blasting as I have said can be used to just matten a glazed surface or to give interesting all over texture to clay but with the use of masks all kinds of effects are possible.

The masks removed revealing the matt and eroded glaze contrasting with the shiny glaze.

Masks

The abrasive grit will easily eat away any hard surfaces but it will take some time to damage soft ones as the velocity and therefore its biting is greatly reduced on contact. For this reason, masks made of a soft material are the ones to choose. All materials will be damaged in time so for work that requires prolonged application of the blast several masks of the same shape may be required so they can be replaced as needed. Cardboard, paper, tapes, plastic sheet, felt, carpet, rubber either as sheet or applied as a latex, and some metals can all be used to varying degrees of success. With metals,

lead and aluminium are best. I have found that using old litho printing sheets that are readily available from your friendly local printer work well. These are thin aluminium sheets that can be easily cut with a strong sharp knife or good scissors and can also be formed to fit the contours of the work. Latex is also very versatile and it would be my first choice to start with.

The masks can either be stuck in place or hand held as long as the arm is sufficiently protected. The general rule seems to be that the finer the grit, the thinner the mask can be so things like masking tape can be quite useful. It is the edge of the mask that usually abrades first and if the definition of the edge is of paramount importance, then several masks will be needed for best results. The softer the object being textured, the quicker the grit will abrade. This in turn means less damage to the mask and hence a crisper edge. Latex would be fine for dry clay, masking tape for bisque or glaze and metal for bisque and fired glaze.

Drawbacks to using masks

There are some major drawbacks to grit/blasting masks. The velocity of the grit and air from the gun is so high that it is very easy for the mask to be blown from the surface. It must be either well stuck down or quite rigid. Masking tape, for example, will stick slightly to dry clay and is useful for several processes already covered but it lifts immediately with grit, so the grit bleeds under the edges and any crispness is lost. However, it works well on glazed surfaces.

If the cut to be made is deep, then once the clay surface being eroded goes below the level of the mask it will then begin to erode sideways under the mask. The result can be that fine lines disappear leaving the mask flapping in the air. The solution is to make masks for deep cuts considerably wider than the final requirements.

The gun should be held at 90° to the surface of the work to reduce the possibility of the grit working under the mask and lifting or peeling it off.

Having said all this, very interesting results can be found in all mistakes and inappropriate uses of materials and techniques.

Final comment

In all the experiments that I did the most successful material for masking was latex and by using it in the form of Copydex in tubes as described on page 39. I achieved what for me were the most pleasing results. Some of the results are shown in the photographs. The rubber allowed long time exposure to the grit which seemed to just bounce away, while the Copydex was little affected.

I have known of the possibilities of grit blasting for some years but was unable to find anyone who used it extensively in their work. With what results I achieved for the research for this book, this is definitely a technique waiting for someone creative to take up.

Chapter Thirteen
Recipes

Rimas VisGirda (USA)

White Engobe Cone 05
Kaolin (EPK)	720
Ball clay (OM4)	720
Nepheline syenite	900
Flint	1080
Borax	180

Black Engobe Cone 05
- 1 pint white engobe
- 3 tablespoons cobalt
- 4 tablespoons red iron oxide
- 4 tablespoons black iron oxide
- 5 tablespoons maganese dioxide
- 4 tablespoons black glaze stain
  (if available)
- 2 tablespoons kaolin
- 2 tablespoons ball clay

Dave Roberts (UK)

Resist slip for 1000°C firing
Flint	2
China clay	3

By volume
Plus 10% copper oxide.

Raku glaze to fix resist slip 1000°C
Borax frit	45
High alkaline frit	45
China clay	10

Carolyn Genders (UK)

Slip recipe fired to 1160°C
- 33% white earthenware clay
  (same as clay body)
- 33% potash feldspar
- 33% ball clay (Hyplas 3354)
- 10–20% lead sesquisilicate

To the slip add 10–15% for strong colours – more than 15% does not increase density of colour. Varying the percentage from 0.5 to 10% will give different shades of one colour. When using oxides 0.5–6%. The carbonates give a smoother colour.

Pliable wax
- 66% wax
- 33% petroleum jelly

Heat together and use hot

Preferred latex wax: from Clayman, Pagham, Nr. Bognor Regis, Sussex.

Sutton Taylor (UK)

Example glaze for lustre 1120–1140°C
Oxidation
Lead bisilicate	33
Calcium borate frit	18
Potash feldspar	25
Zinc oxide	2
Quartz	14
Body clay (Earthenware)	8
Tin oxide	8

The optimum temperature for reduction for lustre is 750°C in gas and 730°C in wood firing.

Example 2 for lustre 1060°C Oxidation

High alkaline frit	90
Kaolin	7
Zinc oxide	3

This is a very soft glaze and the optimum temperature for lustre reduction is 630°C

Clay mask plus lustre salts

Kaolin	95
Gum Arabic	5

The proportion of metal salts can be anything from 5% metal 95% clay to 40% metal 60% clay with good results.

List of Suppliers

T.C.A.S, Spraying Equipment
Unit 3
46 Mill Place
Kingston upon Thames
Surrey KTI 2 RL, UK

Tel: 0181 546 1108

Suppliers of all types of compressors, sprayguns and extraction equipment.

Manco, Inc
830 Canterbury Road
Westlake, Ohio 44145–1462, USA

Tel: 800 321 1733

Suppliers of a wide range of adhesive tapes and films.

Duncan Enterprises
5673 E. Sheilds Avenue
Fresno, CA 93727, USA

Tel: 209 291 4444

Suppliers of a wide range of pottery supplies and interesting colours.

Potclays Ltd
Brickkiln Lane
Etruria,
Stoke on Trent ST4 7BP, UK

Tel: 01782 219816

A wide range of clays and general ceramic suppliers. I use their water-based wax which I have found the best for my uses.

Amaco Inc
4717 W. Sixteenth Street
Indianapolis, In 46222–2598, USA

Tel: 317 244 6871

A wide range of interesting colours colours for all uses.

Brick House Ceramic Supplies
Cock Green
Felsted, Essex, CM6 3JE, UK

Tel: 01371 820502

A wide range of ceramic supplies including a range of ready to use masks, colours and good waxes.

Reward-Clayglaze Ltd
Units A,B & C
Brookhouse Industrial Estate
Cheadle
Stoke on Trent ST10 1PW, UK

Tel: 01538 750052

A wide range of colours as well as general pottery supplies.

Griffin Manufacturing Co Inc
1656 Ridge Road East
P.O Box 308
Webster, NY 14580, USA

Tel: 716 265 1991

Manufacturer of the 'Griffhold Dual Cutter' and a wide range of specialist craft knives.

Index

Note: page numbers in italic refer to illustrations